MINIMA PHILOLOGICA

WERNER HAMACHER

Translated by CATHARINE DIEHL AND JASON GROVES

Fordham University Press *New York 2015*

"Ninety-Five Theses on Philology": This work is reprinted from "95 Theses on Philology" (*Diacritics* 39.1 [Spring 2009]: 25–44). Excerpts from it were published on invitation by Jonathan Culler and Cathy Caruth in a special edition of the *PMLA* (125.4 [2010]: 994–1001). It was originally published by Urs Engeler as Roughbooks 008: Werner Hamacher, *95 Thesen zur Philologie* (2010).

"For—Philology": This work was originally part of a lecture series on philological questions organized by Jürgen Paul Schwindt at the University of Heidelberg in 2002–3. It appeared in the published version of the colloquium *Was ist eine philologische Frage?—Beiträge zur Erkundung einer theoretischen Einstellung.* Jürgen Paul Schwindt, ed. (Suhrkamp 2009: 21–60). It was also published independently by Urs Engeler as Roughbooks 004: Werner Hamacher, *Für—die Philologie* (2009).

Fordham University Press has no responsibility for the persistence or accuracy of URLs for external or third-party Internet websites referred to in this publication and does not guarantee that any content on such websites is, or will remain, accurate or appropriate.

Fordham University Press also publishes its books in a variety of electronic formats. Some content that appears in print may not be available in electronic books.

Visit us online at www.fordhampress.com.

Library of Congress Cataloging-in-Publication Data available online at catalog.loc.gov.

Printed in the United States of America

17 16 15   5 4 3 2 1

First edition

MINIMA PHILOLOGICA

IDIOM INVENTING WRITING THEORY

Jacques Lezra and Paul North, series editors

CONTENTS

MINIMA PHILOLOGICA

NINETY-FIVE THESES ON PHILOLOGY

—Translated by Catharine Diehl

1

The elements of language explicate one another. They speak for that which still remains to be said within that which is said; they speak as philological additions to one another. Language is archiphilology.

2

The elements of language explicate one another: they offer additions to what has hitherto been said, speak for one another as witnesses, as advocates, and as translators that open that which has been said onto that which is to be said: the elements of language relate to one another as languages. There is not one language but a multiplicity; not a stable multiplicity but only a perpetual multiplication of languages. The relation that the many languages within each individual language, and all individual languages, entertain to one another is philology. Philology: the perpetual extension of the elements of linguistic existence.

3

The fact that languages must be philologically clarified indicates that they remain obscure and reliant upon further clarifications. The fact that they must be expanded philologically indicates that they never suffice. Philology is repetition, clarification, and multiplication of impenetrably obscure languages.

4

To be able to speak means to be able to speak beyond everything that has been spoken and means never to be able to speak enough. The agent of this "beyond" and of this "neverenough" is philology. Philology: transcending without transcendence.

5

The idea of philology lies in a sheer speaking to and for [*Zu-sprechen*] without anything spoken of or addressed, without anything intended or communicated.

6

The idea of philology, like the idea of language, forbids us from regarding them as something had [*eine Habe*]. Since the Aristotelian definition of man as a living being having language uses the (linguistic) category of having [*Habe*] for language itself, and thus tautologically, language is without a finite object and is itself a non-finite category, an *apeiron*.

7

The object of philology is—in extension and in intensity (reality), as well as in the intention directed toward it—infinite. It lies, as Plato might say, *epékeina tes ousías*. It is therefore not an object of a representation or of a concept, but an idea.

8

From the *logos apophantikos*, the language of propositions relating to finite objects in sentences capable of truth, Aristotle distinguishes another logos, one that does not say something about something and therefore can be neither true nor false. His only example of this nonapophantic language is the *euche*, the plea, the prayer, the desire. Propositional language is the medium and object of ontology as well as of all the epistemic disciplines under its direction. Meaningful but nonpropositional language is that of prayer, wish, and poetry. It knows no "is" and no "must" but only a "be" and a "would be" that withdraw themselves from every determining and every determined cognition.

9

Unlike the sciences—onto*logy*, bio*logy*, geo*logy*—that belong to the order of the *logos apophantikos*, *phil*ology speaks in the realm of the *euche*. Its name does not signify knowledge of the logos—of speech, language, or relation—but affection for, friendship with, inclination to it. The part of *philia* in this appellation was forgotten early on, so that philology was increasingly understood as logology, the study of language, erudition, and finally as the scientific method of dealing with linguistic, in particular literary, documents. Still, philology has remained the movement that, even before the language of knowledge, awakens the wish for it and preserves within cognition the claim of that which remains to be cognized.

10a

In contrast to philosophy, which claims to make statements about that which itself is supposed to have the structure of statements, philology appeals only to another language and only toward this other language. It addresses it and confers itself to it. It does not proceed from the givenness of a common language but gives itself to a language that is unknown to it. Since it does this without heed and *à corps perdu*, it can remain unknown to itself; since it seeks a hold in the other language, in the one that appeals to philology, it can assume that it recognizes itself in this language. Out of a language of unknowing, it springs into a form of knowing. It defines itself as the mediation of nonknowing and knowing, determines itself as the bearer of the speech of the same to the same, becomes the methodical procedure of the securing of epistemic orders, and furthers—against itself—their hegemony. Philology loves and in the beloved forgets love.

10b

The privileging of predication over plea, of propositional knowledge over wish, of topical language over the atopical, can be reversed neither by a violent act of knowing better nor by utopian wishes. But philological experience is recalcitrant. It shows that the desire for language cannot be restricted to the forms of knowledge. Since it is itself the advocate of this desire, it is close to the conjecture that forms of knowledge are only stations of this desire, not its structure.

11

If all propositions are not only capable of addition but also in want of it—be it only in their demand to be heard, understood, answered—then propositions belong to a language that for its own part is not structured as proposition but as claim, as plea, wish, or desire.

12

The languages of knowledge are grounded in languages of non-knowledge, epistemic practices in those of the *euche*: ontology in philology.

13

Poetry is the language of *euche*. Departing from the other, going out toward the other that *is* not and is not *not*, *phílein* of a speaking, addressing, affirming without likeness, unlike itself: impredicable.

14

Poetry is *prima philologia*.

15

That philology is founded in poetry means, on the one hand, that the factual ground for philology's gestures and operations must be found in the structure of poetry—and that it can only thereby lay claim to a cognition that would do justice to it; on the other hand, it means that philology cannot find any secure, coherent, or constant ground in the structure of poetry. It must, therefore—albeit as an advocate for the cause of poetry—speak with another voice than that of poetry: as divination, conjecture, interpretation. Its *fundamentum in re* is an abyss. Wherever there is no form of proposition, there is no ground of knowledge.

16

The two languages of philology—the language of longing and the language of knowledge of longing—speak with each other. But the second can only repeat [*wiederholen*] what the first says; the first can only overtake [*überholen*] what is said by the other one. In this way they speak each other, speak themselves asunder, and speak their asunder.

17

Philology is not a theory in the sense of an insight into that which is. Nor is it a praxis that is led by a theory or that has a theory as its end. It is—if it *is*—the movement of attending to that which offers itself to this attending and which slips away from it, encounters or misses it, attracts it, and, attracting it, withdraws from it. It is the experience of drawing into withdrawal. The movement of a search without predetermined end. Therefore without end. Therefore without the without of an end. Without the without of ontology.

18

Every definition of philology must indefine itself—and give way to another.

19

The formula of the human being as a living being having language—
zoon logon echon—can be clarified by the modification: he is a *zoon
logon euchomenon*—a living being appealing for language, longing
for it. He is a *zoon philologon*. His longing for language is a longing
that exceeds every given language. His cognition of the given one
cannot do without the experience of its giving and its refusal; his
exploration of the finite one cannot do without the opening of an
infinitely finite one.

20

Where knowledge is missing, affect stirs. Where ontology stalls, philology moves.

21

Philology is the passion of those who speak. It indicates the angle of inclination of linguistic existence.

22

There is no philologist without philology in the most original meaning of the word. . . . Philology is a logical affect, the counterpart of philosophy, enthusiasm for chemical cognition: for grammar is doubtless only the philosophical part of the universal art of dividing and joining (Schlegel, *Athenäum* frag. 404).

23

"Logical affect," in Schlegel's etymological elucidation of philology, may mean affect for language but also affect of language, thus affect of language for language. If language turns toward language, if it is inclined toward it, then toward itself as another, as one distinct from it. It joins with itself as another, departed from it or ahead of it, solely in its affect, its "enthusiasm." Philology can mean a "universal art of dividing and joining" not because it attempts to neutralize the dividing through a joining but because only through division can it join itself with that from which it is divided. Philology is inclination not only for another empirical or potentially empirical language but for the otherness of language, for linguisticity as otherness, for language itself as perpetual alteration.

24

Philology, phil*allo*logy, phil*a*logy.

25

Once again, otherwise: philology is the inclination of language to a language that is, for its own part, inclination toward it or to another. Philology is therefore the inclination of language to language as inclination. It likes in language its liking, language's and its own. Language is self-affection in the other of itself.

Philology can only like and like itself because it is not philology itself that likes and that it likes. It is each time another that likes, each time another that is liked. Thus it will even like its dislike and its being disliked. It is philology of its misology.

26

Philology is language in three [*selbdritt*]. In four [*selbviert*]. The fourth wall of the scene of its relations remains open.

27

What is most proper to language, no one knows: that it merely concerns itself with itself. That is why it is such a wonderful and fruitful mystery—that if someone merely speaks in order to speak, one pronounces precisely the most splendid and original truths. . . . Out of this arises the hate that so many earnest people have against language. They notice its willfulness . . . (Novalis, *Monologue*).

28

Since it has no power over language and none over itself, philology cannot be structured as the reflexive self-consciousness of language. It is from the outset beside itself. It forgets itself. Since it gives itself over to its cause, language, it must allow itself to be forgotten.

29

As the forgetting of language belongs to language, so the forgetting of philology belongs to philology. Only in virtue of its self-forgetting can philology pursue language without subsuming it under the form of knowledge; only because of its self-forgetting is it disposed to assume the form of a science and, more precisely, of ontology; only in forgetting itself, however, is it also historical and susceptible to change: always to another language, always to another form, always an-ontologically.

30

In Plato, there is still no separation between philologos and philosophos. Later, philologos is the one who takes from books, philosophos the one who takes from himself. . . . Towards the end of the fourteenth century and in the fifteenth century. . . . One was at once a jurist, physician, theologian, etc., and philologist (Nietzsche, *Encyclopädie der Philologie*).

31

There can be no history of philology that would not be a history from philology. And no history of philology and from philology against which philology would not have its reservations. As it exceeds every given language, so philology—in additions and precisions, doubts and demands—exceeds every representation of its own history. It transforms the given into the movement of giving and releases this giving from a reservation.

32

Narration proceeds sequentially. It combines discourses on events, actions, and states of affairs through an express or implicit "and then." Even if a sequence adopts the form of addition—if it turns the "and" into a "plus," the virtually infinite series into a finite sequence, and this, in turn, into an aggregate or an ordered totality— "and then" always remains the minimal formula for the combination of assertions, the temporal copula for the generation of a storyline. It is the task of philology to exhibit this construction. Thus, its task is also to exhibit in this "and then" a "thereafter," in the "thereafter" a "no longer," and in the "no longer" a "not." Connectives are not so much placeholders as place openers for a "not." Only this "not"—be it as "no longer" or as "not yet"—allows for the possibility of a story by preventing the sequence [*Folge*] from withering into an inference [*Folgerung*]. Before every and in every "therefore," which maintains the causality of actions and the motivation of decisions, stands an "and then" and a "not" that provide neither a *causa* nor a cause and thereby indicate that history is only that which takes a "not" as its point of departure.

33

What touches a "not" is contingent. Thus, history can be called contingent. It takes place where something breaks off and starts [*aussetzt*].

34

What happens is parting. [*Was geschieht, ist Abschied.*]

35

The inner law of language is history. Philology is the guardian of this law and of this one alone.

36

It is the task of philology to perceive, realize, and actualize in every "and so on" a "not so on," a "not and," and an "other than thus." That is the smallest gesture of its politics.

37

Philology is love of the *non sequitur.*

38

The fact that philology turns its attention to the constellation of phenomena, to the configuration of figures, and to the composition of sentences indicates that it is no less interested in the dark ground out of which phenomena, figures, and words take shape than in these themselves. For that ground is their sole "co" or "con" or "cum."

39

For philology, language does not exhaust itself in the sphere of means. It is not mediation without being at the same time a leap, not transmission without being at once its diversion or rupture. And thus also for philology itself: chopping copula, chopula.

40

Plato investigates the concept of *philia* under the title *Lysis*. Philology: loose attention. Should not that *philia* thereby loosen itself and dissolve?

41

Alois Riegl noticed a change in the construction of space in late Roman art, decisive for history ever since; he characterized this change as the "emancipation of the interval." This phrase is also the formula of philology. Philology emancipates the interval from its border phenomena and, going a step farther, opens up phenomena out of the interval between them, phenomenal movements out of the aphenomenal in their space in between, space out of a fourth dimension: in the end, every dimension out of the nondimensional.

42

"M'illumino/d'immenso" (Ungaretti). The incommensurable does not lie outside of language. It is language.

43

Since language exceeds itself infinitely and discontinuously, the end of philology must be the leap of language.

44

The name has no name. Hence it is unnamable. (Dionysios. Maimonides. Beckett.) Two extreme possibilities of philology: philology is a life that completes itself as the spelling of the name and therein cannot be pinned down by any nomination. It thus becomes sacred and a matter of lived theology. Or: language is treated as a sentence-language in which none of its elements touches the name because all elements are dispersed into sentences. The philology of sentences claims to be profane.—Since one cannot speak in nominations about the life in the name, one must be silent about it. Since profane philology knows no name but only an infinite play of sentences, it has nothing essential or hyperessential to say. Common to both philologies is that they say nothing about their nonsaying. It remains for an *other* philology—one that does not conform to the opposition between the theological and the profane—to say even this nonsaying. Or is precisely this what is already happening in both? Then theology would practice the integral profanation in the extreme; profane philology would practice the theologiza-

tion of language—and both would do so by articulating in the ano-
nymity of the name an *atheos* and an *alogos*. It would fall to that
other philology to elucidate this movement more than the first two
philologies could wish.

45

In the course of secularization, Sunday—the Sabbath, the rest-day and holiday—was abolished; the work day became every-day; the everyday and workday language became the lingua franca; philology changed from a medium of the unfolding of the sacred to a toll for working on a happiness that is neither to be found by means of work nor in it; it became—that too—a branch of an industry producing linguistic mass commodities and mass-market-commodity producers. One of the decisive historical questions that a different philology has to pursue is whether or not all of its working days could still fall on a Sunday. Whether or not all of its works, those to which it is directed and those it performs itself, could celebrate the "Sunday of life"—that of Hegel or that of Queneau. This other philology cannot be out for an end and a goal; it can only be out for a feast.

46

Philology: in the pause of language.

47

Philology is the event of the freeing of language from language. It is the liberation of the world from everything that has been said and can still be said about it.

48

If language speaks for a meaning, it must also be able to speak in the absence of meaning. If it speaks for an addressee, then it must also be able to speak in the absence of an addressee. If it speaks *for* something, it must also be a "for" without a "something" and without the particular "for" that would be predetermined for it. Only one half of language is an ontological process; philology must, therefore, also concern itself with the other half.

48

49

Language is the *objeu* of philology.

(With a philologist's ear, Francis Ponge heard in the word *objet* the different *objeu* and used it in his texts. He thereby wrote, as Joyce did on a larger scale and more deliriously in *Finnegans Wake*, another philology. *Objeu* is the object that preserves in play its freedom not to ossify into the object of a subject. It is the counterplay against the objectification of a thing by naming it. Each word, and language as a whole, may be such an *objeu*. In the *objeu*, language plays against language.)

Philology—which, like all language, is a language about language and therefore the play of its unpredictable movement—is language in *trajeu*.

50

Hölderlin's *Giebt es auf Erden ein Maaß? Es giebt keines* ("Is there a measure on earth? There is none") refuses Protagoras's claim that this measure is man. Anthropology cannot ask about man because it thinks it already knows that man is the unshakable certainty of the subjectivity of the subject and as such the measure of all things. Anthropology knows, in short, because it does not ask. But asking about man exposes this certainty to a language that offers no measure of man and thus no measure of anything at all. Hölderlin says that the sorrows of the one who asks—Oedipus—are *indescribable, unspeakable, inexpressible*. The disparity between language and the unspeakable, between expression and the inexpressible, leaves language without measure, without *metron*. For this reason, Hölderlin's language speaks in "free rhythms."—To a language, that is not attuned to itself and therefore cannot be "correct" [*stimmen*], corresponds only a philology that finds no measure, whether traditional or contemporary. A philology in "free rhythms."

51

There is no metalanguage that could not be disavowed by a further one. This disavowal is one of the gestures of philology.

52

. . . er dürfte, | spräch er von dieser | Zeit, er | dürfte | nur lallen und lallen, | immer-, immer- | zuzu. | | ('Pallaksch. Pallaksch.') (". . . he could, | if he spoke of this | time, he | could | only babble and babble | over, over | againagain. | | ('Pallaksh. Pallaksh.')")—How does philology answer these verses of Celan? By refusing all attempts at measurement through a norm of language that shatters in them. By recognizing that the psychiatric diagnosis of these verses as manifesting an aphasic disorder is itself a disorder of language. By pursuing their memory traces to Hölderlin, Büchner, and others; by following their cadences like movements of diving in traumas; by adopting them as a memorandum of a language that would be human in a different way—a language of pain that can only say that it is allowed to babble but that injures its own law: which does not bring pain to language but language to pain. Language pain: how does philology respond to it? By recognizing it as the pain of its own language? By repeating otherwise the pain of the other? By changing the pain, the other? By letting itself be changed? By releasing it? But the poem poses no question. Philology gives no answer.

53

Language cannot be the object of predicative assertions because these assertions would both have to belong to their object and not belong to it. No trope can designate language without being a linguistic trope and at the same time not being one. Every assertion about language and every trope for it thwarts itself. What is called "language" in language is the an-tropo-logical event par excellence.

Philosophy was only able to do justice to this complication by assuming, since the eighteenth century at the latest, that it is essential to the human being to lack a determination of essence; that his essence, therefore, lies in his existence and that this existence cannot in turn be essentialized. Philology can only do justice to this complication by understanding linguistic existence as an inconsistent event, which is to say as a movement that follows neither the logic of predications nor the logic of tropes without deactivating the one as well as the other. Philology is an-tropology, not anthropology.

54

When Roman Jakobson opposes "the poetic function" as substitution on the axis of equivalences to another—one could say "prosaic"—function that is realized through combination on the axis of contiguities, then the geometry of their relations implies that both axes cross in a zero point at which they follow both a logic of substitution and of contiguity, of poetic as well as of prosaic functions—and also of neither of the two. The rhetoric of metaphor and metonymy, which for a century has occupied philological work in poetological, anthropological, and psychoanalytic studies, relies upon a zero-rhetoric with a zero-function of which not even the figure of prosopopoeia can render account, since prosopopoeia consists in a positing rather than in no positing. Zero rhetoric would be that which marks the empty place [*Leerstelle*]—and, more precisely, the opening for a place [*Stellenleere*]—which is necessary in order to safeguard the possibility of a language at all. Only the philology of the zero would be the *origo* of philology.

55

While philosophy can only concern itself with a *nihil negativum* from which it tries to remove its objects, philology concerns itself with a *nihil* to which every negation must still be exposed in order to be considered as a linguistic occurrence. So little is this a null nothing that it can be characterized as a *nihil donans*. For philology, there is not merely a "there-is-language"; there is also a "there is no 'there-is-language.'" It is language that gives (itself) and language that withdraws (itself, this giving).

56

Topoi also have their time. Philology—which pays as much heed to the usury of tropes in the baroque and in Romanticism as it does to the disappearance of *topoi* in the twentieth century—will notice that the drainage of language, on the one hand, allows predication to emerge as the (ideological) central *topos* and, on the other hand, multiplies a gap—an interval—into gaps—and intervals—that cannot be contained by any *topos* but hold open an a-topy or u-topy. The time of space is suffused with the time of spacing; time spacing is no longer a condition of phenomenality but its withdrawal into the aphenomenal. Time also has its time: it is ana-chronistic.

57

What belongs to philology—besides the inclination to that which is said—is the courage for that which is not.

58

The fact that philology applies itself to detail, to the nuances of a detail, to the *intermundia* between these nuances, slows its movement in language and in the world. Its slowness has no measure. As temporal magnifier, it even stretches the moment and lets leaps occur within it that do not belong to chronometric time. A world without time, a language without time: that is the world, language, as it is—: whole, without being there; exactly this, completely other.

59

Philology—the absolute fermata.

60

Philology is slow, however quick it may be. Essentially slow. It is lateness.

61

"Quand on lit trop vite ou trop doucement on ne comprend rien."
Whoever reads too quickly or too slowly indeed comprehends
nothing, but for this very reason it may occur to him that compre-
hending, capturing, and keeping (*prehendere, capere, conceptio*)
are not genuinely linguistic gestures. (I notice that Pascal wrote *on
n'entend rien*. Too late. Still.)

62

For philology is that venerable art which demands of its followers one thing above all: to step aside, to take time, to become still, to become slow—it is a goldsmith's art and connoisseurship of the word which has nothing but delicate, cautious work to do and achieves nothing if it does not achieve it lento. But for precisely this reason it is more necessary than ever today, by precisely this means does it entice and enchant us the most, in the midst of an age of 'work,' that is to say: of hurry, of indecent and perspiring hastiness, which wants everything to 'get done' at once, including every new or old book—this art does not so easily get anything done, it teaches us to read well, that is to say, to read slowly, deeply, looking back and forward, with reservations, with doors left open, with delicate eyes and fingers . . . (Nietzsche, *Daybreak*, Preface §5).

63

Where philology encounters utterances, texts, or works that are entirely understandable, it will shudder as if it were in front of something already digested, become polemical in order to keep it away, or turn aside and remain silent. Obviousness excludes understanding and even the inclination to it. Only what is disconcerting can be loved; only the beloved that remains disconcerting while growing closer can be loved lastingly. Only what is incomprehensible, only what is unanalyzable—not just *prima facie* but *ultima facie*—is a possible object of philology. But it is not an "object"; it is the area in which philology moves and changes itself.

64

No philology that would not enjoy stillness—that of letters, of images, of architectures, and even of music and of thoughts. Even in the spectacle, it only turns to that which is for no one and nothing. Everything else is theater, on its side no less than on that of its "objects."

65

Et tout le reste est littérature. "And all the rest is literature." Philology has to do with this rest named by Paul Verlaine as well as with that other rest of which it is said in Shakespeare, *The rest is silence*. To distinguish between these rests, these silences—their difference is sometimes infinitesimal—philology becomes critique.

66

The fact that they say everything and mean nothing could characterize works that turned out well. They have no outside to which they refer; they contract the world into themselves. As one says of a stone that it is contracted matter, so are they contracted world. They are *dicht*, *Gedichte* [dense, poems]. For this reason, they are not closed and shut off: they also speak—since they say everything—for others and for other times, but they do not denote them, claim no knowledge of them and none of themselves. The idea of philology that corresponds to *this* monadic structure of works would thus not be interpretation, referring them to another world and placing them in its service, but clarification, saying only that something is there—spoken, painted, composed—or not there. Such clarification comes about only in becoming strange. Philology is the experience of something becoming strange [*Befremden*]. Therefore, it becomes slow and silent; therefore, its counterpart slowly turns into stone. But who is the Gorgon?

67

Philology indeed asks "*Qui parle?*" and does not only ask about a speaker but a perhaps incalculable plurality of speakers and speakers for, speakers with, and speakers after—and it thus asks about "itself." But it asks; and since every question is posed in the absence of an answer, and since this absence can be infinite, it must also ask "Who is silent?" and "What is silent?"—and it must approach itself in silence [*erschweigen*].

68

Perhaps there is only still-life for philology. One knows that such still-lifes can also be battlefields and slaughter-feasts. Everything is still living, everything already still.

69

The exercise of philology—the *askesis*, training, learning, practice, unlearning, forgetting of philology—lies in waiting. It is not always something for which we wait. Before expectation [*Erwartung*] was waiting [*Warten*]. Within it, the presence [*Gegenwart*] of philology expands. It is waiting by the word.

70

Philology: the holding back, holding open. A guard, waiting [*Warte*].

71

Philology is *nekyia*, descent to the dead, *ad plures ire*. It joins the largest, strangest, always growing collective and gives something of the life of its own language to the collective to bring those who are underground to speech. It dies—philology dies, every philologist dies—in order to permit some of those many an afterlife, for a while, through its language. Without philology, which socializes with the dead, the living would become asocial. But the society of philology is the society of those who belong to no society; its life is lived together with death, its language an approaching silence.

72

Philology digs—digs out—the world.

73

The historical "process" is sedimentation, depositing in layers without ground. Languages do not die; they sink.

74

Orpheus is a philologist when he sings.

75

Philology is already, in its first impulse, philology of philology. It distances itself from the myths of philological praxis, does not tolerate any transhistorical constants—transforms Orpheus into Eurydice and her into Hermes . . .—it de-sediments. If everything went according to philology, from the earth and the subterranean nothing would be left over but the free sky.

76

Philology, a love story.—Freud, in a letter to Wilhelm Fliess on December 29, 1897: *Mr. E, whom you know, suffered an attack of anxiety at the age of ten years when he attempted to capture a black beetle* [Käfer], *which did not allow it to happen. The interpretation of this attack has until now remained obscure.... Then we broke off the session and next time, he told me before the session that an interpretation of the beetle has occurred to him. Namely: Que faire?* What Freud, the philologist, calls "interpretation" is not a translation [*Übersetzung*] of a word into a representation of the thing associated with it, but a dislocation [*Versetzung*], a displacement of attention from the possible meanings to the idiom of their naming. Only through separation from meaning does an idea [*Einfall*] take the place of an attack [*Anfall*]: in place of anxiety, its articulation; in place of the animal or the name of the animal [*Käfer*], a question (*Que faire?*). And indeed in another language, French, for—so Freud continues—E's *governess and his first beloved was French; in fact he had learned to speak French before German.* The way to "interpretation" is not the way to meaning. It is the way to a repetition of a language or to a return into a language that is kept hidden by another. The movement of philology is the movement to the language of the first beloved, to the beloved language. The question "Que faire?" and that which is asked by it are allowed to happen this time, in the repetition, by the beloved. For in "Que faire?" that which is still asked about is already done.

Philology: to bring it about that the first love can be repeated, so that it allows the repeating to occur.

77

What is repeated is not the past but rather what of the past went into the future. Philology follows this course and takes from the future what it lacks in the present.—What is lacking to philology?— Nothing is lacking.

78

To the question of what comes *after* philology, one can, nowadays, expect the answer that this would be postphilology. But not only is every (and also this) answer to this question a philological answer—for no one could even begin to understand the question and no one would be capable of an answer without a minimum of philology—even the question is fundamentally a philological one, when it asks about the end and the beyond of philology. From the outset, philology goes beyond to something other than that which it is; it is the way to that which it is not and thereby is—transitively—its not [*Nicht*] and its after [*Nach*]. Its being is nearness, so far as it may be; so near as it may be, the distance. Far-nearing is the time-space that philology opens up and that remains closed to philosophy.

79

Does the pull go from the foreworld to the afterworld or the reverse? Or, at the same time, the reverse? Is not every reversal a repetition? And every repetition an affirmation and an erasure of that which is repeated? Does not every repetition come from another future?

The time of waw ha-hippukh *is the messianic time* (Scholem, "95 Theses," no. 83).

80

Philology is the name for a future of language other than the intended one.

Since it answers for what in language—and in itself—remains intentionless, blank, and unknown, philology is the name for the secret of language, for its *secretum, pudendum,* its home, the wound, for that which does not belong to it and which it itself is not. For its, for one, for no determined gap in ontology and in logic. Therefore a mis-nomer.

81

Current theories of media presume there could be media even if there were no language; language would be a medium among others. This is not so. If there were no language, there could not be a single medium. Language is the medium of all media. They are all, each in its particular way, linguistic: mimicry, gestures, the arrangement of spaces in a building, of buildings in a settlement, the distribution of colors, figures, the framing of an image, technical constructions of every kind. They are built on revocation. They assume that they become destructible, incomprehensible, or misusable, in any event do not arrive at their goal, cannot accomplish their purpose. What determines them—and indetermines them—is not a *causa finalis* but a *causa finalis defecta*. They only function because they could also not function. They all relate to a future that could not be their future, not the future projected in each one's construction, supposed or assumed by them; they relate to their not.

Media are languages because they attempt to anticipate their collapse and even play with the collapse of this attempt. They operate with possible breaks and with the breaking off of their possibilities. That is to say: they operate with their nonoperationality; they mediate their immediality.

Whenever "media studies" begins to make transparent this distructure of its objects and itself, it becomes philology.

82

The ground of philology is a wound. It screams. But no one hears this Philoctetes except, maybe, himself. He is isolated. The men of war first come to his island when they notice that they cannot go further without his bow. (But where are they going to, if not to further wounds?)

83

A passion is a trauma. An insight a stitch. Since philology is the first passion of those who speak, it is no wonder that they do not like it, that they do not like liking it. But in order not to like something, one must like this nonliking. Philology is—ad infinitum—the liking of the nonliking of language.

84

We are, all of us, accustomed to speaking badly of language—*These ambiguous words* (such as "make" [*machen*]) *are like striking several flies with one blow* . . . (Freud, letter to Fliess, December 22, 1897). The disposition to strike and strike dead, which, however subtly, is connected with philology, can hardly be explained other than through the fact that language itself is perceived as brutalization. To reduce massive affects to minuscule noises and scratches requires an expenditure of psychic and somatic tension that easily turns against the desired result of reduction, against language, speaking, the speakers. Logoclasm belongs to language as misology to philology. Instead of fearing an everthreatening collapse of sublimation, one should warm to the thought that language represents an indeed elastic but also exceedingly fragile limit of sublimation that can be broken through at any time through gestures, mimicry, infamies, fisticuffs, and worse. And is broken through in every sentence, every syllable, and every pause. Violence belongs to the structural unconscious of our language because violence channels its way to consciousness. We only insufficiently know what we do when we say something; with some luck, we shall have known it. In the interval opened in this *futurum exactum*, philology moves.

85

The Christianity of philology took an embarrassing turn with its reform in the sixteenth century, which to this day has not ceased in its effects. The divine *logos* of John the Evangelist, at one with love, became a God that hated creation and condemned his believers to spend their lives in *hatred of self* (Luther, "95 Theses," no. 4). The most pitiless consciousness of guilt is thus imputed by a word, a language, a discourse that represents the simple perversion of the *logos* that was still in force in the *philia* of Plato and John. What is said in the phrase *hatred for oneself* is: language hates us, condemns us, persecutes us, and we hate, condemn, and persecute ourself and, in ourselves, language whenever we seek to make ourselves understood in it and about it. (*—Was heißt, haßt.—*) If language hates itself, it seeks to destroy itself, and since it can achieve this destruction in no other way than through silence and action that themselves still claim the value of a language, it can preserve itself only through its repetition in the course of its destruction. What Freud attempts to capture with the concepts of death drive and repetition compulsion is a historical order of misology that strives to extinguish every history, order, and language. Since the reformatory about-face, long prepared for, the intensified interest in the letter that kills; since then, the propagation of the "book" that chastens; since then, the reproductive technologies of the word; since then, the credo of capital, credit; since then, the economy of guilt [*Schuld*] and of debts [*Schulden*]; every word a crime that repeats another in order to hide it. . . . One of the most pressing tasks of psychohistorical philology lies in analyzing this world-historical turn to a sadistic language and to a suicidal philology.

86

The relegation of philology to an ancillary discipline of dogmatic theology, jurisprudence, historiography; its shrinking into a disciplinary technique in pedagogical institutions; its contraction to literary studies; and above all the attempt to force it under the norms of an epistemic discipline: however destructive these institutions of repression were and remain for the experience and clarification of linguistic existence, they have not yet been able to destroy the philological impulse. But one should not deceive oneself: this impulse is destructible. The nationalisms in whose service the national philologies have placed themselves, the juridicism, classism, racism, and sexism that they serve and often uphold are assaults on linguistic and philological existence from which the most gruesome ravagings proceed day by day. These philologies are self-destructive. An*other* philology has to fight with the means of analysis and invention—with all means—against this work of destruction.

87

As long as a single person must *pay* to be able to speak with others and to read and listen to them, language and philology are not *free*.

88

Philology follows the pleasure principle as little as does language. There is no *plaisir du texte* that would not start with repetitions and strive for repetitions. Yet every repetition of an experience also repeats the pain of separation from it—and repeats at the same time the separation from repetition.

Repetition thus not only repeats; it releases itself from repetition and dissolves it. It turns to another beginning, that is to say, back to something other than a beginning. It—philology, repetition—does not only turn back. It begins, without principle.

89

There are philologies that treat the world as if it allowed itself to be *behandelt* (treated like a sick person), as if it allowed itself to be *verhandelt* (negotiated with like an enemy), as if it allowed itself to be *handeln* (traded like a commodity or traded with, like a business partner or an instrument), as if it allowed itself to be *abgehandelt* (handled like a theme). They forget that philology is not a part of the world that can trade with or act on another part. It is the movement of its becoming a world: the coming to the world of this world. This coming does not allow itself to be made, to be bargained for, to be achieved through intentional acts. The nonnegotiability of this coming (of this world) is the experience that another philology has to elucidate. Its provisional maxim: act such that you can leave acting. And further: act without a maxim, even without this one.

90

Philology fights in a world civil war for language and for the world against the industrial manufacturing of language and of the world: it fights against muteness. It must therefore be prepared to fight against its own tendencies toward industrialization. One of the most fatal, most soporific, most disaffecting forms of this tendency is journalism.

91

Philology is the Trojan horse in the walls of our sleeping languages. If they awaken,

92

Hölderlin's philosophical and poetic attention is condensed in a philological remark that is related from the time of his misery. It says, "Look, my dear sir, a comma!" One could call this remark a philographic one if it were certain that every comma adopts a graphic shape and that "comma" in fact means comma. If one considers the weight that the future, the arrival, the coming claimed in Hölderlin's language, then this "comma" may also hint at that which is not asserted but is called and invited to *come*. Philology would then be attention to that which interpunctuates, brings to a hold, creates caesuras, because within it something that comes—or its coming—becomes noticeable.

93

If philology were conducted by all and with unlimited candor—so one could think—then murder and manslaughter would rule, and soon there would be no more language and no more philology. But language places distances between speakers and into their worlds; in a conversation between two, it always refers to a third and a fourth, and if it allows "persons" to come to speech, they do so as those who stay in language and hold themselves back within it. However deadly language can be, it is first of all nothing other than the interdiction to kill. Language is the taboo about death, about the *totum*, the totem. Philology is not only the guardian of this taboo; in each of its gestures, it invents it anew.

94

Philologists also dance around the golden calf, around the gold standard of culture, around the cape of good hopes: cattle and capital dances. The point, however, is to dance the dancing. (Marx, *Theses on Feuerbach*, no. 11)

95

To write—thus, philology—*as a form of prayer* (Kafka). It is only possible to pray if there is no God. Only the prayer yields a God. The perpetual bifurcation between none and one is the path of philology. It is an ongoing aporia, a diaporia.

95 seqq.

The delight therein: that the indefinite slowly defines itself.

FOR—PHILOLOGY

—Translated by Jason Groves

There is an antiphilological affect. More and more among the human sciences, philology is seen as a petty, narrow, elitist, and in extreme cases hostile enterprise of specialists who presume to practice as a profession what any literate person does naturally. This affect—hostility toward concentrated attention to language, words, pauses—turns into defensiveness and often to disdain across a wide public, and the affect is also shared by many philologists, fueled as it is by energies closely related to those of philology. For philology, no matter how entrenched in the academy, is not a discipline. It is not only or even primarily for scholars and pedagogues. Even before academics can lay claim to it, philology must already be practiced by anyone who speaks, anyone who thinks or acts by speaking, and anyone who attempts to bring to light and indeed to interpret his and others' actions, gestures, and pauses. Whoever speaks and whoever acts, in order to be able to speak and act, does philology, even if it is called by another name. For in the sphere of language nothing is self-evident, and so much needs elucidation, commentary, and elaboration. Philology always finds something further to add—

to the particular as well as to the universal. Above all philology is what it futhermore also is; it is "in addition to" itself: the extender, the augmenter, the appender, which no saying or happening [*Gesagtes oder Geschehenes*] fulfills. And what is more, philology goes above and beyond; it runs ahead of and gets behind every existing statement or text, in order to show its movement out of heretofores and hereafters [*Herkunft und Zukunft*]. Philology is the gesture of a "furthermore" that can never be superfluous because it is the movement of speaking itself, overriding everything already spoken and still to be spoken. Philology, for which the most general things must become a problem, is the supergeneral: a longing for language, for everything grasped by it and everything it could still touch, a longing that recoils from every totality, and which, speaking for another and yet another, critiques everything that has been achieved and can be achieved. Since even our agreement on the meaning of concepts—the "general," the "particular," the "special," and the "idiosyncratic"—depends on commentary, philology must be the one thing that does not come under any concept but nonetheless that which no concept can do without. Philology is the precarious movement of speaking about language, above and beyond every given language. It does not guarantee knowledge but renews its postponement, does not offer consciousness but indicates manifold possibilities for its deployment. Even before it solidifies into an epistemic technique, philology is an affective relationship with—a *philia*, a friendship with or befriending of—language, and moreover, a relationship to a language with no firm contours, no consistent form, and not yet an instrument of meanings fixed in advance. A groping, seeking, and probing movement, philology is not primarily the agent of statements about stabile states of affairs; it is rather a prime mover [*Movens*] of questions. Just as little as there are, for philology, linguistic facts, it is not a settled fact that statements or communications deliver on their intentions or arrive at their addressees. Philology assumes that significance and communicability [*Bedeutsamkeit und Mitteilbarkeit*] can only take place if, *before* every determinate signification and *before* every completed communication, philology restricts its movement *on behalf of* them. Philology is the advocate of this restriction, *for* which and *through* which there can be language in the first place. It must therefore defend itself against its own prevailing definitions, while at the same time protecting itself against every agenda for its future practice.—Philology poses questions, and when it makes claims it is only to invite further questions. It is a structurally ironic procedure that not only suspends individual linguistic utterances—even those that are called philological—but furthermore suspends the purportedly "whole" world of language, in order to lay open another that has not yet existed. For this reason philology maintains a mobile relationship to other linguistic complexes, in particular to the so-called exact sciences, on principle an unprincipled, anarchical relationship; for this reason philology plays the trickster or joker in all humanistic disciplines, and for this reason the special power and peculiar impotence of its relationship with these disciplines appears most starkly in its inclination toward poetry. Poetry is first philology. Whether it knows it or not, every philology takes its measure from poetry's world-openness, its openness to this and every possible world and to impossible worlds as well. It takes its measure from poetry's distance and attention, its sensitivity and receptivity [*Empfindlichkeit und Empfänglichkeit*]. Philology speaks for a "for" that makes room for a *pro* as much as a *contra*. Beyond both, it is the movement through which they can be questioned, through which philology itself and its questions can be put into question.

When you are unfamiliar with something and you feel you should turn your attention to it to get to know it, you will ask yourself— or someone else—what it might be, this thing. You can pose this question, explicitly or implicitly, only when the unfamiliar object of your question is already there, even obtrusively there while at the

same time unfamiliar and inaccessible. This singular circumstance—
a thing singled out as both obtrusive and inaccessible—corresponds
to the linguistic form of the question, *what might it be?* [*Was das
denn sei?*] For the question directs itself toward something—to a
this, a *das*, a *quid*, or a *ti*—without being able to follow its path to
the end and grasp the ultimate object of inquiry. Just as the thing
that provokes this kind of question is simultaneously obtrusive and
inaccessible, every question that responds to this provocation is itself an obtrusive, often impertinent, and yet obstructed approach to
its goal. Nothing changes in this internal division of the question if
the object of inquiry is a linguistic construct rather than a thing—for
example a sentence—or an institution made out of language, such
as an appointment, a law, a complex communicative relationship,
a society, or a "culture." Nothing changes in the double movement
of the question when it directs itself toward those institutions—
philology, for example, or philosophy—that pursue the analysis—
and thereby also the question—of language. In all of these cases,
question and thing remain in the balanced relationship of a face to
face that ensures their interrelation as well as their distance.

This distance dissolves and the balance between demands is lost
if the question and the act of questioning themselves come into
question. Of course, a questioner can turn away from the most in-
trusive and obtrusive object and comfort himself with the supposedly familiar and certain, thereby ceasing to be a questioner. But the
moment that his question turns upon itself, drawing every element
involved in its genesis, including the questioner, into its vortex, the
questioner can no longer turn away. Whenever a sensation, word,
institution, or a pattern of discourse becomes simultaneously unfamiliar and obtrusive, the resulting astonishment and wonder can be
diminished or eliminated only where the questioning takes the form
of goal-oriented research—a *query*, a *quest*, an *inquest* and investigation—of the enigmatic phenomenon. If the act of searching itself
is not investigated, if the question does not inquire into itself, it can
still offer at least the semblance of a stabilizing effect. The search
becomes a fixed formula, and the question becomes a paved path, a

method, a procedure. As much as it might appear to unsettle things, the question—of who or what something is, of its structure or essence—is always also a gesture of protection in which the form of the question safeguards itself. Once it is more than just a phenomenon that is in question, once the path of access to the phenomenon, the path governed by the question, becomes the problem, then it is no longer only the "who" or "what" that is placed in question: every possible question—even the question of ground and goal, of sense, meaning, and form—every "why," "what for," "how," and therefore the very form of the question itself is placed in question, such that even the minimum certainty afforded by wondering and searching is shattered. In this catastrophe of questioning—which is simultaneously a catastrophe of language in the act of questioning and a catastrophe of language in general—the form of questioning itself and not an external thing has become both unfamiliar and obtrusive and hence provokes the question concerning it. Yet this self-provocation of questioning coincides with its self-obstruction; to the extent that the question remains unavoidable because obtrusive, it also remains cut off from itself because unfamiliar. In the question regarding the question, in the peculiar structure of a self-provocation—a provocation by an alien or as an alienated self—and in the corresponding structure of self-obstruction or self-protection—protection against an other or an altered [*Verandertes*][1] self—it becomes discernible that the question "itself" is split, duplicated, in itself an antagonistic complex. Insofar as the question concerning the question takes place, it becomes inaccessible to itself.

Whoever asks the question "What is a question?" can hardly doubt *that* he does something or lets something called "questioning" happen, but he will probably be in the dark as to *what* it is supposed to be that he does or lets happen when he asks this. He asks about an unknown *what*, in which the *that* of its fulfillment is supposedly stabilized into an object. What the question ought to be is a movement toward an unknown something, but now the unknown something resides in the question itself, and the movement that should have led to something else is now directed toward the movement itself—and as such it reveals that the movement is indeed completed, but precisely for this reason it cannot be made into an object of its own cognition. The question still asks what the question already is. But in just this way, *that* the question still asks *what* it already is, it attests at the same time that the question in its *thatness* precedes every attempt to arrest it in a cognitively comprehensible *what*, and as such the question exceeds every objectification. The peculiar aspect of questing *after* the question consists in the fact that in every here and now it is *ahead* of itself, and thus divided from itself it also falls short, fails to correspond to itself, each time running out ahead of its truth—conceived within the correspondence theory of truth—yet also lagging behind it in a sheer, answerless, responseless and correspondenceless search [*Suche*], an insatiable addiction [*Sucht*], and only in this way remaining with itself. In the pure *that* of its asking, the question concerning the question is ahead of itself with itself as though with another.[2] What a question might be is therefore an impossible question, in the sense that it exceeds every possibility, every capacity or faculty, and every power to comprehend itself, while it exists alone as sheer self-*excendence*. The question exists not by transcending itself toward a commensurate other but rather by going out of itself and beyond itself and ultimately transiting toward itself as an inconceivable other—and thus perhaps to a not-other—and remaining in transit. The event of this *excendence*—of questioning—does not let itself be reduced to a substance, be it the ultimate object of inquiry, the questioner, or even the question form, for such a substance could only lie in this *excendence* out of the question and therefore only in an unforeseeable becoming-other [*Veränderung*]. The question concerning the question is, like all questioning, pressing [*dringlich*], but it is set apart by an objectless and never sufficiently thematized pressure [*Drängen*] that slides beneath its preservation in a "what" or an essence. Because questioning can take on no finite form—and so no form at all—that cannot be questioned and thereby set out of action, it is possible that these movements are also at work in the apparently simpler forms of predication or of the imperative. Pure questioning is always more than each question that can be posed; it is hyperteleological, unlimitable, endless, and it could only find its answer in itself—if that answer [*Antwort*] were the kind that withheld from itself every word [*Wort*].

Since there are questions only in language—be it a language of gestures, conduct, or social organization—the question concerning the question is in each of its movements a question concerning language. Because beyond this the question is not contingent but rather at work like a virus in each and every linguistic and language-tinged relation—linguistic relations reach a climax in the question but never a conclusion—; because the question is not "logical" but rather investigates the structure of the logos, a structure it courts and at times harasses, this single question is the *philo*-philological question *par excellence*. What, then, can be made of the question "What is a philological question?"? If the question concerning the question is the fundamental or, more precisely, the a-fundamental philological question, then the question concerning a certain question type, classified as "philological," can be understood not only as a limit on the question concerning the question but moreover as a distraction from its significance as a question. Up for debate in the "philological question" is a technical, disciplinary problem, already defined and also always requiring further definition; this debate has preestablished historical parameters and only allows for procedural answers internal to the discipline. But the question concerning the philological question can be understood in still another sense. That is to say, this question implies that philology defines itself in the first place through its questions and thus neither by means of a particular range of objects nor by means of what used to be called "worldviews" and what are now known as cultural presuppositions, convictions, or beliefs. Furthermore it implies that a path to what in a strict sense can be called philology can only be embarked upon by the question concerning the philological question. Such a question makes possible an emancipation from the *doxai* of other disciplines, from techniques of knowledge, and from modes of experience, thereby allowing it, at least in principle, to detach from the stock of a tradition that has become questionable and that over the course of its history—for the most part under the tutelage of juridical and sectarian or antisectarian convictions—has defined its borders. Whatever a philological question may be, it does not first of all inquire into the contours of a well-established academic discipline—if it were established in that sense, the question would have been settled—nor does it look for opportunities to stabilize this discipline against hostile takeover by other, allegedly more profitable ones. For then the question, wondering how to support a collapsing order, would become a Baron von Münchhausen: urging us to support the collapsing order on the basis of the same order. The order does not lend itself to being "supported"—this is implied in the question, what a philological question in general might be. Perhaps it is not "worth" being supported, perhaps it has no "significance" that could justify its continued existence. Whenever there were such significances, values, or normative authorities in the history of philology, they were—or so one could imagine—exclusively borrowed from the more renowned neighboring disciplines. Only in exceptional cases were these values and meanings critically examined by philology. From its earlier status as an *ancilla theologiae et iurisprudentiae*, philology became an auxiliary branch of historiography, sociology, psychology, cultural anthropology, and the history of technology, and it generally submitted to the objects of attention, perspectives, and methodological imperatives dictated to it—not always to its disadvantage but seldom to the benefit of its critical power.

Philology's *servitude volontaire* is not a thing of the past. Even when not self-incurred [*selbstverschuldete*], its peculiar form of immaturity [*Unmündigkeit*] was not a mere weakness in the past, nor is it one in the present. For philology is the form of being assigned to [*Angewiesenheit*] language and assigned first of all to the language of others, to expressions, spoken and written, fleeting and archived, expressions that in turn stem from other—be they ascertained or uncertain—sources, from others' texts and, as a rule, from

texts that for their part reply to still other texts. Because philology
depends on others, it readily understands itself as a mode of reference [*Hinweisung*] and a medium and means for those others, yet
it just as readily misunderstands itself as agent of a meaning that
is said to lie stored, openly or encoded, in that other, in the utterance, declaration, or text toward which it turns its gaze or which
is forced upon it. In this scenario philology does not present itself
as lover and friend of the word but rather as a dutiful repetition of
a more powerful, guiding, dictatorial meaning, just as a child re-
lates to a knowing adult. Philology's word is the minor child [*das
unmündige Kind*][3] who finds its determination at the knee of an
adult meaning [*der mündigen Bedeutung*]—but the child in its arms
is dead. It is dead because its language is merely a derivative of a
meaning and because at the place where this meaning is captured
and fixed in an institution, philology's word can be erased. Again
and again philology has aided and abetted the death of the word
in meaning, insofar as it has put itself in the position of the *infans*
with respect to the all-powerful matrix of meaning. This death of
philology in the mother-text [*Matertext*] is the—very real—consequence of the phantasm of semanticism, which says there are origi-
nary and self-sufficient meanings. Such meanings do exist, but not
as naturally occurring or transcendental givens; rather, they arise
out of the play of linguistic structures that operate in relative inde-
pendence from what they could mean. Whoever grants this much
can still claim that there are historically alternating and, to some
extent, regulative schemata of meaning, and on this basis they can
try to make it sound plausible that language, and with it philology,
always performs its work according to a normative authority and
therewith ceases to exist. But they would be left to explain how
those quasi-transcendental historical transformations happen and
out of what immanent tensions and deviations they spring. And so,
they would have to concede at the very least that linguistic practices
do not fully merge into meaning and that the experience of language is never thoroughly determined by its service to schemata of

the understanding. Even if only a single element of language—for example the question—escapes a historically regulated regime of meaning, then the guardianship [*Vormundschaft*] of the norm over language is broken. When the presumption that there are meta- and mother languages collapses, philology can no longer orient itself toward the norms, perspectives, and methods of other disciplines, and it certainly cannot raise any of these to the position of a model discipline. To be sure, the experience of philology is characterized by a constitutive dependence [*Verwiesenheit*] on the language of others, yet this must not imply a simple co-dependence or symbiosis; its needs cannot be satisfied through subsumption into an already established horizon of meaning. The entrance into horizons and the blending of horizons spell the death of language, not its birth. For a child to die in his father's or mother's arms, the child must already exist, as must the *philia* or *eros* that drives it. A child is more than the dumb extension of its predecessors and guardians. It is a *novum*, another kind of inception and the inception of another kind. So too for every word and so too for its advocate, philology: they must, in order to be able to speak for others, themselves begin to speak.

One of the difficulties determining what philology is stands out in the question concerning its peculiar way of questioning. This difficulty [*Schwierigkeit*]—this *difficultas*, awkwardness, adversity, and even the impossibility of its taking place—stands out in the fact that the question is always posed anew and that it can never be answered out of context, that it can never be answered without consideration of the particularities and singularities of its actual and possible objects, and so it can never be answered succinctly. Every question, no matter how urgent, leaves open the possibility of being unanswerable. A question that did not refuse an immediate answer and accept the possibility at least for an instant that it might be unanswerable would not be a question but rather a heuristic instrument for the extraction of already available information; it would be an exam question and one that in turn did not deserve to be examined. If we recognize that the question concerning philology, and thus the question concerning the relationship to the word, is already a relation to a *pending* word and to a *pending* and perhaps impossible answer, we also recognize that the question refers to a more illuminating answer, one that does more justice to the object and to the question than any other readily available answer could. Philology's embarrassment at lacking an answer to the question of what it does is not merely the passing malaise of a discipline that awaits its definition and thereby its redemption. Embarrassment at not knowing and perhaps never knowing what it does *is* philology. This becomes more explicit when, rather than furnishing the question concerning philology with a provisional answer, one poses the counterquestion: from whom, from what authority, and with what right can this question even be posed? The question thus presents itself: can philology pose this question? Can a philologist, in so far as he speaks as a philologist, pose this question?

To ask what a philological question is is to ask what is philological about a question and its object. It is to ask what makes philology "philology" and thereby to admit that you do not know, or that you have reasons to mistrust its traditional claims to knowledge. This question is not posed by a scientist who can already account for the substance and principles of his activity but rather by a researcher, thinker, or analyst who attempts to sound out the basic principles and the determining form of a praxis that does not offer him knowledge—at least not the kind regulated by concepts—about what philology does, whom it pursues, to what it directs its attention, and by which question it is guided. The question concerning the philological question and thereby concerning philology is therefore not a scientific question, although it can be understood as a question concerning whether philology is a science. Thus understood it already contains, *as* a question, the answer: it isn't one. Were there fundamental principles of philology, as a science, then the question *about* philology would not be allowed to belong *to* it, since questioning indicates nonknowledge or not-yet-knowledge.

However, not only knowledge but even methodological access to knowledge is placed in doubt by the question concerning the question. Merely taking into consideration its questionableness [*Fraglichkeit*] shows that philology is neither a science nor a theoretical discipline with a well-defined procedure that would lead to the acquisition of knowledge. Because of this, the question concerning philology can at most aspire to be a propaedeutic and therefore a protophilological investigation. It is not a question for a science of philology but rather—*sit venia verbo*—a question for a philo-philology that is detained at the border, the drawbridge, or the portico of philology but that does not enter into its interior and does not know its law. It is therefore neither a technical nor a disciplinary question, and it does not belong to the methodological arsenal with which a science of language fortifies itself and within which individual linguistic or quasi-linguistic phenomena solidify. This is not to say that this question or the one who poses it must behave indifferently toward philology. On the contrary: the one who lingers at the margins of philology will perceive its contours more sharply than the one who claims to reside in its interior and is thus deluded into thinking that certain defined procedures can pass for philological ones. To inquire philo-philologically into the practices that are called "philology" does not only sharpen one's view of them; it also sharpens an experience inseparable from philology, when we take it at its word. This is an experience of *philia*, an inclination, an emotion that intensifies in the philo-philological relationship to philology and that, as a movement *toward* philology, itself ushers in the movement *of* philology. The question concerning philology testifies to the fact that philology can neither be a primarily cognitive praxis nor follow a primarily theoretical interest. As a question of *philia*, it also testifies to the fact that philology is an affective attitude, an inclination toward language and toward all phenomena proximal to language and falling outside the scope of phenomena, a turning toward and an approach that finds no foothold in the knowable and that therefore moves in the passages—even if they are infinite—of one language to another language and of language to something other than language. The question concerning philology diminishes our knowledge but enhances our affection.

*Phil*ology is a *patho*logy. That its *pathos*, the *pathos* of *legein*, is traversed by a double movement, that philology always makes the experience of nearing simultaneously into the experience of a distancing, and the experience of turning toward something into the experience of having turned away from it—this double movement emerges with particular clarity where philology is forced to see that neither its objects nor regulated access to them falls under its control: namely, in the philo-philological question that can neither be avoided nor answered. Its pathos is a pathos of dis-stance [*Ent-fernung*]. On the path toward the reference of a linguistic expression—a signification, a form, a meaning—philology is referred onward to something else—a complex of forms, the signature of an epoch, an idea—to things that themselves, also linguistically constituted, also carry the sequence of references onward. The nearer philology comes to its object of concern, the farther it withdraws. Its reference is a reference to the withdrawal of reference. Therefore its *philein* is never simply the relationship of same to same, of mere concordance or correspondence, without at the same time being a relationship of distancing, suspicion, and turning away. Not only occasionally, and not because of the peculiarities of those who practice it, but rather on the basis of the double movement of language, philology maintains the closest affinity with *misology*. This too is a response to the removal [*Entfernung*] of that which attracts it. From the constant disappointment an aversion to language can grow among routine practitioners of philology, an aversion that easily leads to disdain and condemnation, to marginalization, and toward a sadistic disciplining of its own practices and self-image. Constructing an epistemic system evades the constitutive re-moval of the *logos* and its *philia*, avoids the praxis of *pathos*, abandons the search for a science of consciousness, while relying on practices from the so-called exact sciences. An addiction to language

[*Sprachsucht*] and a flight from language [*Sprachflucht*] are the counterstriving tendencies that move philology; philology is also the only praxis that can articulate and analyze both tendencies without betraying either. Only philology can pose the question of what a philological question is because philology alone can endure the absence of a binding and conclusive answer. The question becomes intolerable only when philology misunderstands itself as a discipline of knowledge, when it limits its scope to a definite subject area—even if it is the most exposed area: poetry, literature—and defines itself as literary science; the question is the most intolerable when it serves theories and methods of knowledge that make language a means to take flight from the question, where language is used to domesticate or to denounce the question of the philological question.

What drives philology is the question concerning it. This is the longing for language, for *language about language*—language as an object and language above and *beyond* each of its objectifications— in which language on the one hand thematizes, objectifies, and defines, and on the other hand is emancipated as an unthematizable, objectless, and addresseeless movement of alteration [*Veranderung*] into another language and perhaps into something other than language. For this reason there is no contradiction between the assumption that the question concerning the question is the philological question *par excellence* and the other assumption that it is a philo-philological question, a prephilological question. Philology is first of all nothing other than the question concerning language and the relationship to language, a question that operates within this very question concerning the question. It searches for itself in what has been differentiated from it. Philology sets out toward itself as toward another, yet only this alterity affords the specific relationship that bears witness to language. Ahead of itself yet behind itself, after itself in both senses: the *philia* of the *logos*, in the tension of the relationship, is the experience—the impassioned experience, the *pathos*, the *passio*—of not ever yet being already that which it could still become, and of being always more than it already is. It is the passion both to speak in a language other than that which it addresses *and* to be addressed in a language other than the one it means to speak.

Philology is therefore first and foremost the experience of being both *exposed to* and *provoked by* language. He who answers is not the one who expresses himself in response to a communication but the one who poses the question whether it even is a communication. He answers with a question—and first and foremost does nothing other than answer, even when his question leaves open whether the object of inquiry is something or nothing. A question answers—and it remains first and foremost questionable whether this answer can be, without further qualifications, a consciously and intentionally directed act [*Tun*] within given conventions of acting—whether it can be a linguistic act classed with so-called speech acts—or whether for the moment it is nothing more than the *inauguration* of an act not yet subjected to the control of an already constituted subject or even to a consensus regarding the rules for acting. To ask is to answer, even with this question, to a claim that *affects* [*angeht*] you, because it *evades* [*entgeht*] you, a claim that urgently or menacingly demands your attention because it itself is not self-evident. You respond with your question to something that does not correspond to your habits, knowledge, and expectations; to something that has no distinct intelligible voice and that, insofar as it bursts the horizon of your ideas of the world and of the language-world, renders you speechless. To question—and to speak—is to answer [*antwortet*], that is, to become answerable to that which withdraws the word [*das Wort*]. This provocation, to which one can respond or perhaps only react, has the disconcerting structure of demanding something [*etwas zu fordern*]—a word, a statement, a usage—in such a manner that this something—precisely this word, this statement, this usage—is refused. If speaking and, above all, if questioning is a response [*Antwort*], then it is a response to the with-drawal of the word [*ein ent-ferntes Wort*] and thus a response to a *provocation*—to a challenge [*Herausforder-ung*], a stimulus, a shock, or merely a touch—through something that itself does not have the character of a morphologically, seman-tically, and pragmatically well-defined *vox*.

An answer [*Antwort*], even if it is taken to be a question, must always also be an answer to *no* word [kein *Wort*]. It is a fragment in a relation whose second element is still to come, and it is therefore always a relation and irrelation at the same time, a relation to an irrelation, a deregulated and disoriented relation to the search for the missing element in which it could complete and stabilize itself. The answer, but also the question, is an attempt at nursing the le-sions on language. And therefore it is an answer to that which is not anticipatable but rather unregulated and in every sense of the word *contingent*. To be touched [*tingiert*] without already know-ing by what or why, to be affected by the possibility that the only one who could possibly speak is the one who refuses a language that is clear and distinct, the possibility that what can be brought to speech is only that which leaves a conceptualizing, thematizing, and regulating language speechless: this is the *pathos* and the passion of philology. And philology shares this *pathos* with everyone who speaks or writes, a fortiori with the poets, who speak of nothing other than the experience of an openness of language [*Sprachof-fenheit*]: of the possibility of language under the conditions of its improbability, of the potency of language under the conditions of its impotence, of power in the horizon of its withdrawal. Poetry is the most unreserved philology, and only for this reason can it at-tract the privileged and arresting attention of philology.

Whoever wants to learn further about the structure of philology will do well to turn to those for whom the meaning of language is the least certain and to those most familiar with the indominability [*Unbotmäßigkeit*] of language. One of the rare authors who, fa-vored by a certain political-philosophical constellation, became the most involved in the structural problems of philology, moves far in this the direction. He does so as philologist of the word "philology"

and as a follower of Plato, who lets his Socrates be designated an
aner philologos (236e) in a conversation he holds with a young man,
Phaidros, who has likewise fallen in love with a *logos*—a speech—
and moreover in a speech about eros, an *erotikos logos* (227c). Plato's "philologist" is a friend and lover of speech about love that is
itself loving speech. He is a philo-philologist, because for him the
logos is already love and moreover the love of love. Language loves.
Whoever loves language like the philologist loves it, loves the love
in language. In the tradition of the Platonic "Phaidros," Friedrich
Schlegel understands philology as affect, indeed as logical, as the
affect of the *logos*, which is for its part oriented toward the *logos*,
toward language. In Athenaeum Fragment 404 he writes: "There is
no philologist without philology in the most original meaning of
the word . . . . Philology is a logical affect, the counterpart of philosophy, enthusiasm for chemical knowledge: since grammar is after all
only the philosophical part of the universal art of dividing and joining."[4] And in the sketch "On Philology" ["Zur Philologie"] of 1797,
Schlegel writes: "Doesn't the deduction of [philology] as a logical
affect and the necessarily subjective conditions for the fulfillment of
the logical imperative break new ground?"[5] And: "reading means to
affect oneself [philologically], to delimit [philologically] and determine oneself. But one could probably do this without reading."[6] And
in the "Philosophical Apprenticeship" ["Philosophische Lehrjahre"]:
"It remains eternally true; as affect and as art [philology] is the fun-
dament and propaedeutic and everything for history."[7] In the way
that talk of self-determination and self-limitation is tied to Fichte,
talk of autoaffection is tied to Kant and his definition of the autoaffection of the mind as the form of time production. Therefore—
that is, out of transcendental-philosophical motives—philology, as
affect, can be for Schlegel the *foundation* for historical time and its
representation in historiography. Autoaffection, taken as philological, is the affection of the logos through itself, its self-touching and
self-arousal [*Selbstreizung*], which would not be possible without a
rip [*Riss*] in it. "No one," Schlegel writes, "understands himself, in

so far as he is only himself and not at the same time another. For example, whoever is at the same time a [philologist] and a [philosopher] understands his [philosophy] through his [philology] and his [philology] through his [philosophy]."⁸ The autoaffection of language is therefore necessarily a polemic with itself as with another, just as it is a polemic with others as though with different selves.⁹ Philosophy in particular is in need of philology because without the affect and enthusiasm of philology, philosophy would wither away to the mere description of grammatical structures of the logos and would not be capable of following that *logical imperative* that leads above and beyond all naturally occurring and conventional rules, thereby entering into the movement of language. Philology is for Schlegel philo-polemo-logy. It is the waging of a conflict that gets played out in the interior structure of the logos. If language affects itself, this is because its "self" is split off through a *krisis*, a cutting off and separating out precisely from this "self" as from "another," and in doing so language engages in permanent *critique*— the explicit disassociation and exclusion of the one "self" from the other, of the one language from the other. Autocritique—and more precisely: heterautocritique, fundamental polemics, transcendental dissensus—is the uncircumventable form of the autoaffection of language and of the logical affect that Schlegel recognizes as philology. Since philology generally determines the blueprint of language, it must assert itself in every linguistic expression and every expression about language. Whoever speaks, speaks about language, addresses language, answers it, and speaks therefore as a philologist. In speaking *about* language you also speak *with* it as though with another, an opposed other, disputing it as an alternative to your own language, and this struggle is itself the unavoidable and interminable movement in which language is constituted. Philology exists as a specialized form of knowledge and as an academic discipline only because it exists by and large as the general form of speaking, whether *to* or *about* the one spoken to. Speaking—even in the mode of questioning—is answering, and every philology is a philology of the answer. However, since philology's answer directs itself to an other language—and *in extremis* to something other than language—and since language is confronted in this other with an alternative or controversial philology, philology's answer, even though it is a movement of *philia*, must also be a—polemical—answer, an antiword [*Anti-Wort*], a counterword [*Gegenwort*], that potentiates the diversity of languages and philologies and at the same time seeks to bring about an agreement between them.

Schlegel's schema of philology as a transcendental-critical self-relation is admittedly extremely formal, but precisely for this reason it can easily be related to the mundane activities that count as professional philology: the critical emendation of traditional texts bequeathed to us, the constitution of an authorized corpus and its commentary and interpretation. In such textual-critical and hermeneutic procedures, a linguistic faculty—that of differential marking—acts on the expressions of another faculty of language—that of repetition and combination or synthesis of markings—and presents in a prosaic praxis the process of autoaffection in a language corpus: to let speak once again what was once said and what has already been repeated differently. But whereas textual critique and its praxis of interpretation and emendation has the objective to establish a correct text and recover *what was said*, for Schlegel and his concept of philology what is at stake is not an inventory [*Bestand*], a condition [*Zustand*], or an object [*Gegenstand*] but rather the movement that gives rise to such a state [*Stand*] in the first place. For Schlegel it is a question of the affect of *speaking*—texts originate in this affect—and it is also a question then of what instigates speaking. Philology is the instigator, as a "logical affect." Language is not system but process, and one that propels itself beyond the permanent self-secession of speaking. If the critical-hermeneutic constitution of a text depends on cyclically turning back to its first or authentic form, Schlegel's affect-philology, in contrast, consists in entering into and surpassing the movement of the cycle. "A complete polemic," he

writes, pointing to a decisive element in philological praxis, "must
parody all manners, crush all corners, cut up all lines, explode
all cycles, puncture all points, tear open all wounds, uncover all
bruises and weak spots."[10] All lines, all cycles, all points—thus the
entire geometry that sets calculable limits to language, the entire
logometry that fixes language into certain figures of succession, figures of the "return into itself" and figures of arrest into a distinct
form—must be *crushed*, *cut up*, *exploded*, *punctured*, *torn open*,
and *uncovered* by the autopolemics of language, which is to say, by
philology; they must be, in a word, *parodied*. These lines, cycles,
and points exist. No philology can challenge their facticity, for they
are facts not only of language in general but also of a philological
autoaffection—both self-limiting and, by disassociating itself from
others, self-determining—in which language perpetually springs
forth. Thus no philological work can refrain from turning its attention to these figures, both the geometrical ones and the rhetorical
ones with which they ally themselves; what is more, philology itself
will have to become a praxis of the geometrization of language:
linear where it synthesizes, cyclical where it reconstructs, and ab-
stract where it establishes points of demarcation. But the process
of production cannot come to a standstill in the geometric figures
produced and reproduced by philology; the work on these objects
has to continue even after they are generated, and the determining
and delimiting affect has to turn, at its limits, into another affect, an
affect of destruction and explosion, that is to say, an affect of the
opening of already posited historical boundaries of language. As
polemic, philology carries the process of language formation forth
[*setzt . . . fort*]: it exceeds every *status quo*, it exceeds the *status
ante corruptionem*, and it hyperbolically exceeds every fixable status. Philology is the polemically generative parody of its objects,
the continual [*fortgesetzte*] self-parody of language. Every language
posits [*setzt*]—structures, functions, and meanings—and every language *sets forth* [*setzt fort*]. And like language and *as* language, so
too philology.

That philology posits and sets forth, however, says that it also follows two verbal gestures, at least these two, which are not independent from each other and not reducible to each other:

On the one hand philology defines a textual corpus according to its boundaries, its belonging, its internal and its liminal structures, as well as its "pragmatic" structures, according to the tropes that traverse it and the meanings that it generates; philology determines lesser or more comprehensive linguistic complexes—individual utterances, idioms, motifs, genres, epochs, national literatures—according to their forms, functions, and operations; philology posits borders and thereby posits, implicitly or explicitly, the rules according to which it prefers these positings.

On the other hand, philology sets these positings forth and carries them on [*setzt diese Setzungen fort*]: it repeats them but changes them in the repetition, generates border conflicts in microscopic and macroscopic regions, causes collisions between single idioms, draws attention to the narrow-mindedness of national and period literatures, and finally directs its critique against the narrow-mindedness of the totality of that which, in manageable historical fields, counts as language per se and literature per se. Philology directs itself against the supercomplex of language with its colliding but in principle definable structures, functions, and operations. That philology sets its positings *forth* and carries them onward thus means: it distances them from one another by pitting the necessity of philology's repetition ad infinitum—the necessity of an infinity of which every linguistic totality can only be a fragment—against both the entirety of language and the totality as defined by philology. Philology is principally concerned with the entirety of all linguistic operations, yet its totality, in the unforeseeable sequence of its repetitions and variations, can only be a fragment of its infinity. Philology, inasmuch as it proceeds definitionally, indefines.

To sever *all* lines, to explode *all* cycles, to puncture *all* points: this means nothing less than suspending the totality of linguistic positing. Schlegel characterizes the mode of this suspension, in the first formulation of his note, as parody: *a complete polemic must parody all manners* . . . However, a parody of the totality of all linguistic utterances, all figures, functions, and operations of literature and language can in no way find an Archimedean point outside the linguistic and literary universe that would give philology leverage on this totality: even this Archimedean point would belong to the totality and, according to Schlegel's aggressive formula, would have to be "punctured." The *stigmé* would have to be re- and destigmatized. If there is a parody of the linguistic totality, and if philology is this parodistic transtotality, then it is so only as the immanent doubling of a language of structures, functions, and operations through exactly the same language without structures, functions, and operations. This repetition would be the parody and para-ode of the satyr play as well as the counterword and antiword of the parabases, which Schlegel knew from the comedies of Aristophanes and through whose procedure he characterized irony, one of the most decisive concepts of his thought: "Irony is a permanent parabasis."[11] Irony, polemic, parabasis, and parody are for him linguistic procedures that permanently accompany the totality of all linguistic constructs, but in distinction to those constructs, these destructural procedures neither have an autonomous function nor lay claim to a semantic content, and they do nothing other than deactivate, asemantisize, and defunctionalize the acts of the linguistic totality. Philology does precisely this. It is the escort of language and of the entirety of its productions, but it itself says nothing and produces nothing of its own. It is the mere medium in which this entirety *exposes* itself: in which it exhibits, introduces, and presents itself [*sich austellt, vorstellt, darstellt*]. But whenever philology analyses, restitutes, contextualizes, and systematizes the entirety of linguistic constructions, each time it does so at a distance within which all of what it posits are suspended [*alle ihre Setzungen außer Kraft gesetzt sind*] and in which its totality is *ex-posed* [*ex-poniert*]: abandoned, cut off, suspended. Philology as Schlegel understands it in no way practices its structural critique of totality as a partisan toward literature, nor does it make a case for a merely regional linguistic competency or content itself with the services of a merely regional science. It does not carve out fragments from an existing totality but rather makes the totality itself into a fragment of an infinity over which philology exercises no power. For philology and for philology alone there is more than everything. For philology there is not only more than what has been imagined but rather more than what is imaginable, anticipatable, and feasible. "Fragments from the future" is what Schlegel names the works that open themselves to philology, fragments from the future that can draw nearer only by way of the immanent suspension of any particular attainable totality.[12] For this reason philology is the advocate of history in literary works. By relating the totality of literary works to that which it is not yet, philology contributes to their historical transformation. Progressive universal *poesy* becomes progressive strictly through the polemic that a corresponding universal *philology* carries out along with it. Philology, understood this way, is the *epoché* of the historical language-world—even its own—for the benefit of another world. It empties out every given language in order to make room for others. But because it makes nothing other than room—philology is decreation—it is the medium in which all languages can speak but which itself says nothing other than the beginning of saying. Like parabasis and parody, philology is a paralogy in which the logos merely continues to speak [*fortspricht*] but does not signify.

Language posits and sets forth, and in doing so it sets out; and so too philology. The two principles of a linguistic event—to posit and to suspend all positings [*zu setzen und alle Setzungen auszusetzen*]—relate asymmetrically. What is posited is posited each time as something said with, in principle, determinable meanings and functions, but what is said relies on a saying that for its part can operate in principle without meaning and without functions. Without mere speaking there is no possibility of saying something. Yet this mere speaking [*dieses bloße Sprechen*] and speaking onward [*Weitersprechen*] does not impart something and does not impart it to someone. That the contents of speaking are not identical to speaking, and that the mere utterance—the phatic act of which the linguists speak—precedes and exceeds every semantic or structural content, becomes most conspicuous in repetition and its variants: in the relatively affirmative ones like rhyme, refrain, and echo, as well as in the subversive ones like echolalia, glossolalia, parody, and the polemical citation. In these something is indeed said that was already previously said, but it is said without letting itself be associated with convictions, claims to validity, or affirmations of meaning. What is said is rendered inoperative in the mere act of saying it and continuing to say it [*Fortsagen*]; everything that Félicité's parrot repeats in Flaubert's "A Simple Heart" is stripped of its meaning in its mechanical repetition. Echo, citation, mirrors are no harmless utensils for the beautification of an appearance. They are the instruments of an evacuation, a dispossession, and a making infinite of what was said in mere saying. Such elements of analytical iteration are legion in language, in particular in the language of literature, and in literature these elements offer models of basic philological operations [*Grundoperationen*]. In them a reflected philology—repeating and retrieving itself in reflection and in this way taking hold of itself for the first time—can recognize what it does and how things stand with its answer to the questions that the texts pose to it.

In a poem by René Char with the title "La bibliothèque est en feu" ("The library is on fire"), one finds the following sentences: *Comment me vint l'écriture? Comme un duvet d'oiseau sur ma vitre, en hiver. Aussitôt, s'éleva dans l'âtre une bataille de tisons qui n'a pas encore à présent, pris fin.*[13]

The three sentences can be rendered as: "How did writing come to me? Like bird's down on my windowpane, in winter. At once there arose in the hearth a battle of embers that has not, even now, come to an end." This text is part of a sequence of aphorisms loosely grouped around a common focus and can therefore be discussed relatively independently from the other *paroles en archipel*, the "archipelagic words" of Char's 1962 collection *La Parole en archipel*. The text commences with the question concerning the coming of writing. The opening question—*How did writing come to me?*—does not question how an "I" came to writing but rather how writing came to an "I." The question itself answers: it provides an answer to the coming of writing, and it could be understood to be, as an answer to the coming of writing, an answer to this same question. The question, how writing came to me, would then be the question concerning the coming of precisely this question, and the question concerning this question would be its first answer. This answer would read: writing came to me as the question of another that repeats itself here and now as my own. My writing is the reply of his writing that has no other place and no other time than that of this reply. The coming of this writing is the collision between "mine" and "his," the strife of question and answer, the *polemos* in speech. These deliberations are confirmed and made more precise in the following sentence, in which each element is repeated and thereby displaced into an approximate homophone: the question particle *Comment* [How] in the comparison *Comme un* [like a], *vint* [came] in *(du)vet* [down], *(éc)riture* [writing] in *vitre* [windowpane], and in this way the question is taken up again and minutely transposed in the answer. Moreover, the second sentence has writing come to the writer like bird's down to a windowpane, in winter. The talk is thus of a touch, the most unobtrusive, gentle, and improbable one thinkable, for birds do not lose their down in winter. The coming of writing has, as a form of "touching" [*Berührung*], the form of what Schlegel calls polemic and what Kant calls an affect or an affection. Even with Char, this affection is no straightforward act of the self touching itself but rather an act of touching a windowpane—that which protects the self against the external world—and an act of being touched by another, more precisely by something that was lost and unintentionally dropped by an other, a down feather. "Windowpane" and "winter" take up rhetorical elements of Mallarmé's poetry, and the figure of the down feather recalls the *plume* that, in the form of a quill, traditionally stands for writing in general. The *pars pro toto* cliché of the plume is diminished, via a metonymic displacement, to a down feather, and this minimal distortion of tradition reduces the image of writing to one of a tender touching, without thereby losing the connotations of writing that have been present since the opening question. The question, how writing came to me, answers itself in this way: it came to me as though to a writing surface that protects me from writing, it came like a collision with my boundaries, and my writing does not merely reproduce this collision but rather is, *hic et nunc*, the event of the collision.

The text grants its question an answer that is nothing other than the rephrased question—it is the question of the other, once again, displaced along the axis of contiguity. I do not write, I am written, and this state of being written continues *even now*, even in that which is written here. The answer that perpetuates the question can therefore be understood not only as a question, for the one writing, of how he came to be a writer. This is equally a question for the reader: *How did this writing come to me?* The answer is in both cases the same: by reading I am written, and so I am the reader of another whose writing continues in my reading. As softly and euphemistically as Char formulates this heteroaffection of writing, in the last three sentences of the text, when the touch of the down feather sparks a firefight, it turns into the most menacing brutality: *Aussiôt, s'éleva dans l'âtre une bataille de tisons*—"At once there arose in the hearth a battle of embers which has not, even now, come to an end." *Âtre* [hearth] thereby functions as a phonetic transformation of *vitre* [windowpane], and the touching of a down feather and a windowpane becomes a beating [*battre*] of a battle [*bataille*] between logs in a fire. Writing, a soft touch by the question of another, becomes a beating, a battle, a blaze. The experience, *I am being written*, is intensified to *I am being lit and set on fire, I am burning and burning up.* The reader, who is a part of this scene because even the author finds himself defined as a reader, comes in contact with this very spark: his act of reading is an igniting, a charring, a blaze. By reading he alights in a firefight inflicted on him by the ineluctable contingency of another.

An apparently harmless, intimate question regarding an almost academic topic (*How did writing come to me?*) has become, through a progressive transformation, the answer that every contact with a word or with a question is a fight and a fire—and even this answer, as it stands, is in flames "even now." It is not a cold question but a burning one, and its fire rages on in the answer. The almost erotically tender affection for a vanishingly minuscule point where the window is touched by the down, where the I is touched by the question, turns out to be an infection that spreads throughout the entire corpus of language, that grabs hold of the reader who stumbles upon this poem, here and now, *à présent*, and that makes presence itself into a battle and a firestorm, an inextinguishable threat, a danger even after minimal exposure. Writing and the question concerning it, reading and the answer that it gives to the word of this question, are *events* that are neither harmless nor harmonious, never strictly intimate, and not exclusively linguistic or poetic; never regional nor bound by a discipline, they are always expansive, carrying on through all forms of contingency and contingent deformations that seep into practices of regionalizing, norming, and disciplining. Although speaking and hearing, reading and writing present themselves as a firefight, the fight and the fire still seem confined in Char's text to the hearth, but since *âtre* [hearth or fireplace] is used in his poetry as a variant of *être* [being], and as fire takes hold even of the writing of which this fire is the subject, its spark jumps over to the entirety of what *is*, of what language is, and what comes in contact with language, setting the totality of the world of language, including the political world, ablaze. *The library is on fire*—the library, and not only the one in Alexandria, but every one, within and without us, is in flames. And with it all the sciences and all the discursive procedures that could be archived by it. Philology burns.

Language and everything coming in contact with it burns and this is no metaphor. It is the metonymic articulation, recurring across contingent relations, of a trauma. In the years of the German Occupation, René Char was the captain of a resistance unit of the Armée Secrète in the south of France. The unit received its supply of arms from the exile government of de Gaulle in London. The arms containers that were supposed to enable the continuation of the fight against the occupiers were dropped before daybreak by parachute out of a plane belonging to the exile government, but during one of these deliveries the first crate exploded upon impact and set the surrounding forest on fire. Char reported on this in his *Feuillets d'Hypnose* [*Leaves of Hypnosis*], the sketches from the Maquis of 1943 and 1944. The unlucky coincidence, which almost cost him and his people their lives, stands in the closest thinkable relation to the brief text about writing as firefight. The designated codeword for the arms drop was in fact called: *La bibliothèque est en feu.*[14] In 1956 Char made this codeword the title of the cited text and the collection of poems in which it is contained. He thereby caused its meaning to multiply: it remains a codeword like any other, and as such it recalls the fight for a life in freedom and demands to continue this fight; it signifies the destruction of everything that was once understood under the terms culture and civilization; it signifies at the same time the possibility that, out of a catastrophic inferno [*Weltbrand*], which may have reminded this Heraclitus admirer of the cosmic fire, another world and another language could have risen like the Phoenix. *L'aigle est au futur*, it says in the same text, *The eagle is of the future.* Finally, the codeword is a witness of the traumatic experience that even the antinomic meanings, and therefore the entire possibilities of meaning of the sentence *The library is on fire*, could be obliterated by an accident, an unfortunate stroke of fate, a stupid coincidence. This poem is also an arms delivery; it too should push the resistance forward, even though it too runs the risk of exploding upon impact, upon being read by its readers—its philologists—and thereby obliterating the resistance, itself, and its password, its *parole*.

The codeword that Char gave his poem as its title multiplies its possibilities of meaning up to the point at which they, in the possibility of the ultimate impossibility of meaning per se, give out. This extreme possibility is the trauma of every language and is passed on by every language. It damages language's most desired ability: to be able to fix and maintain principles, norms, and schemas of meaning in a continuum of communication. The experience of language is always also the experience of the danger of no longer being able to speak; the experience of communication is always the experience of the danger of not reaching an addressee or of destroying him and communication itself. This traumatizing danger is not a vague possibility that could perhaps become a reality; it accompanies speaking and speaking-with-one-another from the outset by determining, *as* this danger, where the stress falls in speaking. And from the outset language is the survivor of this danger and bears its traces.

Language orders, schematizes, regulates, and communicates; however, it can neither determine the meaning nor regulate the wounds in its meanings, rules, and communication: it can only witness them. The senseless accident to which Char almost sacrifices himself and which would have devastated all of his battles and sentences is witnessed in the sentence "the library is on fire"; through remembrance and in its continuing effects it is witnessed—and in being witnessed it is combatted. On the one hand this indicates that the sentence "the library is burning" itself burns, together with everything that belongs to it; it is a part of the burning library and burns with it, even here and now: this "battle of embers . . . has not, even now, died down." And on the other hand it indicates that this sentence is the survivor of its own blaze; it is a part that is, if not larger, then nonetheless other than the whole of the library to which it belongs and other than what is burning, that is, other than itself. It is the remnant that speaks about—outside of—the whole and that speaks out about and even beyond the contingent possibility that nothing can speak any longer. In this sentence two fires are burning: the flames of destruction and the counterflames of resistance. The trauma of the linguistic world repeats itself in this sentence, but it can repeat itself in it only because this sentence has outlived the trauma, because it distances itself from it as a witness, and because it speaks for others, for future languages, for their benefit and sent to their address. The sentence *from* a traumatic past is a sentence *for* another future, but it could not be one if it did not already speak from another future. *L'aigle est au future*: this does not only mean that the eagle is in the future or belongs to the future; it also means that the eagle is in the future tense. Even as it stands here and now, the eagle is the arrival of another time: my window being touched in winter by a down feather, by *his* down feather, the coming of writing, the flare-up of the fire, the burning of the library, philology in flames. Philology incinerates philology to make room for further philologies equally ardent. Its fire is *for* another fire and the "for" of another fire. It stands for the futurity of that which is. What Char writes of the coming of writing, what he writes as a philologist of writing, is induced and ignited first of all by this writing that thereby acts as the witness for another writing. Philology does not work on the sublation of secured meanings in an asbestos institution; rather, it flares up as a protector and witness of the futurity within everything that institutions seek to fix in writing.

If the outline for the basic operations of philology can be recognized in the movements of language, in particular the language of poetry, then at least two things can be said about it: philology, if it is to be a *phil*ology, cannot defend itself with aseptic techniques and immunization tactics—whether these consist in crude historicizations of the type "once upon a time" or in linguistic neutralizations of the type "this is a q-function"—against being affected by language. This includes its catastrophes and its traumatizations, the realia associated with them and the irrealities that traverse those. The language of literature, more than any other, has been understood as a medium of processing and integration for those affects, stimuli, and injuries that proceed without discipline from such a linguistically organized world just as well as from a linguistically unorganizable world. Another language may integrate itself into a closed corpus, become a comprehensive whole or a dense continuum of meanings and relations—literary language does not restrict itself as much in these ways. It is a priori porous, open for contamination and receptive to what does does not assimilate into any form without giving up its aspirations to coherence. If this *literary* language is a definite form, be it an endlessly redefinable one, then it is one that invites the shapeless, the monstrous, and the decomposition or refusal of every form. Literature responds to provocations, but it responds to them not because it can—in which case they would not be provocations—but rather because literature itself and its ability to respond stand in question and because it must seek, find, and invent answers even beyond its capacities. Philology, where it deserves this name, responds to the questions, provocations, and attacks organized by literature *not* when it has an adequate technical arsenal at hand but rather when it is disarmed and must seek for other responses than those at hand. Literature is a feature of language *in extremis*, at the very border where it is bumped into or ruptured by an unregulated, untamed, wild affect or an uncontrollable coincidence.

Philology is not literature; however, it is also not a philology when it is has nothing in common with literature. Philology is an ancillary language to the other language of literature and to virtually every other language. Philology accompanies literature, listens to it—and therefore must often fall silent—and amplifies literature's voices by repeating, translating, and transforming literature passage for passage, fragmentarily, and by placing accents as it goes along. Philology speaks *with* literature, but it speaks in a different idiom than literature. It formalizes, but where it normalizes it cannot follow literature into that region in which it breaks through all norms. Philology thus speaks *with* literature but not as though with an instrument that it places in service of disciplinary practice; philology speaks with literature only by speaking toward it, *for* it, and for the benefit of that which seeks to liberate itself in literature. It is a medium of rearticulation, even for literature's affects, even for its affections produced by the most meaningless and affectless contingencies, and it can therefore, even where it formalizes most severely, never be far from a wild philology.

The responses that philology can give to the provocations of literature are always also responses to the violence to which these provocations, for their part, respond. This violence can be that of a hardly noticeable emotion, persuasion, rhetorical subreption, or insinuation, but it can also be that of a massive threat, intimidation, and brutalization through rhetorical schemata and thematic privilegings. In all of these cases—in the entire spectrum from a lullaby to a novel by the Marquis de Sade—philology can never simply make itself into an agent of this violence. As the medium of their rearticulation, philology, even if it itself exerts a piece of irreducible linguistic violence, is first and foremost the suspension of this violence. In a poem by Paul Celan, first published posthumously, this suspension is addressed.[15] The text stems, as becomes apparent in both its dating of July 28, 1968, and Celan's concurrent reading notes, from a period of intensive occupation with the writings of Walter Benjamin. It responds to them, and it speaks of this responding:

UND WIE DIE GEWALT
entwaltet, um
zu wirken:

gegenbilderts im
Hier, es entwortet im Für,

Myschkin
küßt dem Baal-Schem
den Saum seiner Mantel-
Andacht,

ein Fernrohr
rezipiert
eine Lupe.

AND AS VIOLENCE
unwields, so as
to take effect:

it counterimages in the
here, it unwords in the for,

Myshkin
kisses the Baal-Shem
on the seam of his mantle-
devotions,

a telescope
receives
a loupe.

In "The Early Romanic Theory of the Knowledge of Nature," a chapter from *The Concept of Art Criticism in German Romanticism*, Benjamin investigates the conditions in which, in the view of the Romantics, especially that of Novalis, knowledge [*Erkenntnis*] of objects is possible. He distinguishes as the most decisive of these conditions the reflectedness of knowledge in the object. An object of knowledge exists only when it is the object of its self-knowledge. This is to say, on the one hand, only that which can be seen can see the one seeing; on the other hand, this is to say that only that which can be seen sees itself. Reality, accordingly, does not form an aggregate of monads locked up in themselves and unable to enter into any real relations with one another; rather, it is a reality only to the extent that each of its elements becomes a medium of reflection of other elements and only to the extent that each element incorporates its own self-knowledge or otherwise radiates its self-knowledge to the other elements. Benjamin can thus summarize his reconstructed theory of knowledge in the sentences: "Where there is no self-knowledge, there is no knowing at all; where there is self-knowledge, there the subject-object correlation is abrogated—there is a subject, if you will, without a correlative object."[16] This consideration—which contains a pronounced criticism not merely of Hermann Cohen's philosophy of correlation but equally of the mechanistic variants of a Hegelian dialectic—claims to be valid for human cognition no less than for that of so-called natural things. Even they are capable of knowledge, and even their knowledge is not restricted to what is known through itself. In order to give clarity to this reciprocal determination, one in which, according to the theory of Novalis, even things lacking consciousness participate, Benjamin cites his remark: "that the star appears in the telescope and penetrates it . . . The star . . . is a spontaneous luminous being, the telescope or eye a receptive luminous being."[17]

When Celan writes at the end of his poem, "a telescope/receives/a loupe," he takes up the thought of Benjamin and Novalis—he *receives* it—but at the same time he states it more precisely, presumably with recourse to other sources,[18] to make it clearer that the knowledge in question is an interdependence of both seeing and being seen, that this knowledge is a relation of autoaffection and autoreception, in which the relata are just as enhanced through one another as they are diminished, just as exponentiated as they are depotentiated. If Celan's text here cites the text of someone else and in the act of citing receives it—moreover a text, Benjamin's, which for its part cites at least one other person—then Celan's text presents *itself* as received and recognized by that text, and in this way it participates in a simultaneously generalizing and condensing occurrence of knowledge [*Erkenntnisgeschehen*], in which self and other interpenetrate the other. Through the altered citation of a citation, Celan's text makes itself into a medium of reflection of a philological knowledge, in which the text is itself the object of knowledge. In this movement, however, the text becomes what Benjamin, a few pages removed from the cited passage, calls the "indifference point of reflection" and what Celan, in a poem that dates to the same day as the one about violence undoing itself, characterizes in almost the same way, namely as an "indifference point/of reflection."[19] It is the very point at which reflection, as original autoaffection, "originates out of nothingness."[20] Out of anything other than nothingness it cannot originate because only in reflection is the becoming of an object also knowledge of it; however, both knowledge and reflection must commence absolutely presuppositionless and therefore at what *they* are not and at what *is* not. The *indifference point/of reflection*, which makes contact with the knower in the known and the citer in the cited, is for this reason the very point in which self-reflection, autoaffection, and self-citation are rendered powerless. The enjambment of Celan's verse after "indifference point" even takes this point apart: it is the pause of language and image, the arrest [*Aussetzung*] of their violence, the irreflexive gap from which reflection goes forth. The act of self-engendering *ex nihilo*—it can be interpreted as the self-limitation of nothingness, as a *not* against nothingness—is possible solely as an engenderment out of a state of self-suspension. This is why Celan's poem speaks of the unwielding of violence, of counterimaging, and of unwording as three irreducible modi—having effects, knowing, and speaking—that are to be carried out where they give out.

The verses "And as violence/unwields, so as/to take effect" can be understood not only as formulations of the sentence about suspensory autoaffection from Benjamin's art criticism study. It can also be understood as a recapitulation of a line of thought from his essay "On the Critique of Violence" ["Zur Kritik der Gewalt"], which will be taken up later in his great Kafka essay. Every act of violence, even the highest, must abstain from its exertion and must therefore abstain from itself, if it is supposed to be violence *against* something. If violence were not to *unwield* itself, as Celan writes, it would destroy everything in its sphere of action, including itself. In order to sustain itself, it must restrain itself. From the paradox of a self-annihilating violence results the counterparadox of a violence that *unwields* itself: no other violence could still function because no other would still be a violence *for* something. Violence, if it is real and working [*wirklich und wirkend*], can only be the one that suspends itself for its sake just as for the sake of another, that is, suspends itself *as* itself an other. Only the violence turned against itself *works* [*wirkt*]: not merely in the sense that it triggers effects but also in the sense that it braids, knits, and weaves, like one works cloth, a rug, a text.[21]

From this structural premise the following verses draw the following consequence; in each "here"—and this means the "here" of the poem and the "here" of each of its readings or philological elucidations—the violence of ideas, images, and representations, of verbal images and rhetorical figures must encounter a countervailence that first of all allows violence to be and to take effect. Only the counterimage offers the resistance that makes an image into an image. But this counterimage can not simply be another image that would stand in contrast or in opposition to an already given image; it must be a counterimage in the sense that it opposes the figurality of the rhetorical figure and the representativeness [*Bildlichkeit*] of the image, repeals them, and opens out onto the unimageable [*Unbildliches*] and the nonfigurative. The contestation of pictoriality [*Bildlichkeit*]—and even the contestation of exemplarity and reproducibility [*Vor- und Nachbildlichkeit*], that is, the mimetic and emulatory character—of the images, tropes, and schemas sets in motion the approach of what is no longer subject to the unrestricted violence of vision: the paradoxical image, the self-unforming image [*das sich entbildende Bild*]. The procedure for the production of this image is what Benjamin names *critique*. He writes of it in the last sentences of his study: "This can be illustrated in an image as the generation of blinding in the work. This blinding . . . is the idea."[22] The idea is for Benjamin neither image nor model but rather—as for Plato—the blinding of intellectual vision [*Anschauung*] and the extinction of the image. But to speak of blinding is to operate from within the image that is supposed to be affected by the brilliance and that paradoxically blinds itself. Just as the *idea* obliterates the idea, so "it counterimages in/the here." "Here" is the epitome of the ideal as well as anti-ideal place, where every word takes a stand against itself. Not only Benjamin's paradoxical *image* of the blinding of the image (of the *eidos*, of the work) by the *idea* is in this sense "unforming" [*entbildend*] (or, as Celan puts it, "counterimaging," *gegenbildernd*); the image of the telescope that receives a loupe is also a *counterimaging*. It offers no object but rather the *reception*, the receptacle, the conception, and—given that "receptive" can be used in contrast and in opposition to "productive" and "active"—the story of the Passion in a process of image formation [*Bild-Bildungsprozess*], in which microscopy and macroscopy interpenetrate one another. The point at which the near view is taken up by the far view and at which both intersect is their *indifference point*, which does not allow any other intuition [*Anschauung*] except that of the structure of intuiting [*Anschauen*] itself, no image besides that of the generation of images, and none in which it would not "counterimage." No intuition and no *theoría* can give an account of the registration of nearness in distance, of distance in nearness, because their relationship as the unintuitable and untheorizable must precede every act of intuition and every theory. Only the suspension of vision allows the visible to emerge.

As the image so too the word: only where the word finds a counterword that does not merely oppose it with a contrary morphological or semantic position inside the city of words but rather turns against the word *as* word; only where it turns against its character as a word and against the absolutist diktat of this character, and therefore only where the violence of a word yields to its "unwielding" can it—*unworded*—speak and work as a word. Working and speaking are not possible for the word that is a self-contained and unconnected unity; rather, they are possible only when it speaks *for* something and works *for* it: for another, whether this other belongs to the domain of language or not. The word speaks, in the first place, in its "for" and therefore speaks only as something differentiated from itself and at a remove from itself. Only this turn

away from itself allows the word to become a word; only its unwording in a *for* allows it to speak, and what it says has in each case
the meaning of a for that stands up for another and that stands by
others. Its unwording cannot have the character of a mere substitution of one word for another or of a word for a meaning that for
its part could be indicated by a word. Nor can "unwording" mean
the mere transformation of a word into any action still conducted
by a word. Unwording must affect the verbal and therefore the linguistic character of the word, and it must affect the latter's claim
to be foundational altogether. Even *before* every thought or opera-
tive word, *before* every announced or written word, the linguistic
character must be exposed a priori to another character that is neither conducted by a word nor grounded in one. The principle and
primacy of the logos are rendered powerless for any knowledge,
language, or action with the—*sit venia verbo*—desentencing sentence "it unwords in the for." The "for," for which it speaks, is the
counterword to the ontotheological root word that is postulated
in the *en arche en o logos* of the Gospel of John. In the beginning
was not the word. In the beginning, so that a beginning and a word
would come to pass, there had to be a beginningless and wordless
countermovement under way—an *ent-*, an *un-*, a *de-*—one that dis-
tanced the word from its *arche*, from its ground in itself, from its
domination, from its violence, and from its use. Whenever it comes
into language [*zum Wort kommt*], it does so in each case from and
to a pro-noun, a *Für-Wort*. And even when it is a word for a word, it
is still a word for an *other* word, *in limine* a wordless "word." Even
before its beginning the monarchy of language was abdicated: the
language of "for" is *an-arche*.

The immanent suspension of the word in the word makes it into
an ad-vocate [*Für-Sprecher*] and a procurator [*Anwalt*] for what is
not accommodated in any word. By *un*wording itself [ent*wortet*],
it *an*swers [ant*wortet*] to its own violence through the unwielding
[*Entwalten*] thereof. Celan's "for" is not one preposition among
others but rather the absolute preposition, the one that makes all

others possible in the first place, the prepreposition that precedes all others. It is not a *Fürwort*, the "pronoun" of the grammarians, but rather a *Für* without a *Wort*, a "pro" without a "noun" for which it could stand as a substitute, a "pro" before every noun and even before itself. It is therefore a *Für*, a "pro," a "for" that itself is *no* word but rather one that both actively and passively *unwords*. A word *for* the word—namely for the word and for language in general—itself cannot be a word of language; language must to a greater extent be that which is prompted by the *unworded* and *unwording* "for." As an absolute fore-word it is an ante-word for every other word, every already known word, and every still unknown word. Accordingly, in the "here" of a certain historical language, namely that of German, it is the most radical, the subradical response to the possibility of a future language and thereby to the possibility not only of a language but of an event that exceeds all words and every language. It is a fore-word and an answer that here speaks for something other than here and in this way speaks for the delocalization of all topical organizing concepts. The "for" in Celan's poem is not a word: in it "unwording" takes place, an "unwording" of itself and every other word *for* which it could stand in and before which it could speak. Unwording the entirety of language, the entirety of its functions, and the entirety of its operations, "for" is a word that usurps all others—it is the universal parasite, the parabasis into infinity, the structural parody of the totality of language—but it is also a word that affirmatively stands in *for* all pending words, even for the word "for." Foretelling and forecasting, it frees up space for them, if not nonviolently [*gewaltlos*] nevertheless by unworking violence [*entwaltend*].

"For" is an open vocable, an atopic locus, a prelinguistic and ad-vocatory [*vor- und fürsprachlich*] gesture whose mixture of affection and restraint makes allowances for anything, anything that is language. As foreword, answer, and counterword [*Vorwort, Antwort, Gegenwort*] to everything speakable, "for" speaks not only for the benefit of the unspoken but also the unspeakable. Speaking for another, and still others, and always otherwise, it cannot do other than speak in each case for nothing and for no one. "For" therefore indicates "for" just as it—itself "unworded in the for"—indicates "not-for" and "un-for" [*Ent-Für*]. In "for" language speaks, against even itself, for its muting, not as though this lay outside of it, and not as though a word could ever correspond to this muting, but rather in the way that it abandons itself to the event of its unwording, that it speaks *with*, *from*, and *toward* its silencing. *For*—language—speaks; *for*—outside of language—falls mute: it mutates. "For" is, in every sense and even in that of a *mutum* that cannot be grasped by any word, the mutation of language.[23]

The unwording that takes place *in* and of the word "for" is not decreed by Celan's poem but rather carried out. The neologism "unworded" [*entwortet*] does not only speak as a paranomasia, as a surname, near-name, and byname of "devalued" [*entwertet*] as well as "answered" [*antwortet*]; moreover, it thereby deprives them of the character of standalone words and renders them inoperable by referring to them as merely virtual in the very word—*unworded*—that expresses their suspension. Even "for" does not speak as a single word, not as the nominal unity of a national language; rather it can instead be read as a homophone variant of the French *fur*, as it is used in the expression *au fur à mesure* or *au furet à mesure*. This expression does not only mean "as the case may be" and "to the extent." It also means "correspondingly" [*entsprechend*]—and this "correspondingly" can in turn be transformed, through the reinterpretation of its prefix *ent-*, into an "un-responding" [*ent-sprechend*] and further, as happens in Celan, into an "un-wording" [*ent-wortet*]. "For," the translation of the French *fur*, is the word for a correspondence that simultaneously asserts an unwording. Rather than only asserting this correspondence between correspondence and its unwording, the poem carries it out by presenting itself as the event of a translation and therefore as the word of transition between two different languages. "For" is speakable and audible only to the extent that in it one language corresponds to another, by the word of one language unwording the word of the other. The French *fur* is moreover derived from the Latin *fari*, "to speak." It is the word for the word and for language in general. Through its transformation into the homophonic *für*, this word for the word becomes a word for the transition of one word to another, for a transition in which the one word does indeed give its response to another word but in the only way it can give this response, such that it is neither this other nor itself. The transition between *fur* and *für* unwords the one and the other, the French as well as the German word, in that both contract to a "indifference point/of reflection." For or *fur* is therefore not simply a word for language but rather for the movement between diverse languages that cite and reflect and, in speaking for one another, deprive one another of speech. It is the word for the unwording between languages, for the free *nihil* in which they originate [*entspringen*], following Benjamin's interpretation of the indifference point; it is the word for the empty place, the empty language where diverse languages speak with and for one another and therefore where no single one speaks.

The for-structure of language can be understood accordingly in at least four senses: it speaks in the sense of a *substitution* for another and works as a placeholder and vicariate of this other. Language is therefore a substitute only in so far as it speaks *for the benefit* of this other, stands by it, and stands in for it even where it keeps it at a distance, represses it, or excludes it. As advocacy for the benefit of another, language is always underway toward this other, crossing over to it [*zu ihm hinüber*], and as such is the movement of *transcendence* to another. The being-beyond [*Hinübersein*] in the "for" of language must open out onto that which would be addressed neither as a positive factum nor as a given word, nor even an anticipatable word, but which rather maintains itself in an otherness remote from, though perhaps open to, language. This being-beyond must lead to a vacancy, and, going beyond every addressee, it must be worthy of an unaddressed and perhaps unaddressable one. It must always also be for-nothing-and-no-one, and as the movement exceeding language, as this excendence, it must also be the *unwording* of this movement. Without these four features of its "for," language could not make statements within a predetermined—but how and by whom?—field, but neither could it open up the field of the addressable, nor could it correspond to the otherness, the unprogrammable futurity, and the possible unaddresability of what it addresses. Only in this fourfold sense is "for" the word for a language that does not only register and communicate what is at hand but rather, open to alterity and history, still remains turned toward a word—even one within language—that can be grasped in no word of no language.

If "for" structures the entire movement of language as well as the movement of each of its elements, it does so as the movement of the *philia* that rushes to others, to other things, and even beyond them. And as "for" speaks for a whole and all and precisely for this reason can neither belong to, nor itself be, a whole and all, likewise the *philia* teeters on the outermost edge and even on the exterior of that which it strives toward. "For," as the *philia*, is, in language, the movement of philology. It is a "logical affect," as Schlegel calls it, the affect of language for an other and for something other than language: affection, longing, or a *furor* for it, whether reserved or poised to make the leap, rushing headlong or taking its time, but always beyond. It behaves like Dostoevsky's idiot behaves toward the devotional world of Hassidism; on its border and moved to speechlessness, he lovingly fails to grasp it: "Myschkin/kisses the Baal-Shem/on the seam of his mantle-/devotions." This kiss is the gesture of philology.[24] It touches a seam, an extremity, an outermost, not in the mode of a self-sufficient thought but rather that of a thinking-of, a devotional thinking [*Andacht*]—of another [*an Anderes*]—and of a devotion that for its part is an outermost, a coat or *mantle*: the "matter itself" of philology is such a *to* or *on* [*ein An*]. Before it can define its objects and arm itself with the rules of an epistemological discipline that ensure its cool distance from such objects, philology is already in contact, and *is* the contact, with a matter [*Sache*], that of language [*Sprache*], one that is wrought [*gewirkt*] out of nothing but precisely such contacts, touches, affects, and in turn out of their seams [*Säumen*], out of its seams, and their unravelings [*Versäumnissen*]. It is advocacy for language and for its "for," a remembrance of thinking and of its "of" [*Andenken an das Denken und sein An*]. It is the movement of an of-another and for-another that traverses—as the reverse of the experience of the in-itself and for-itself in a Hegelian absolute knowledge—the movement of an absolute language and of its absolving.

Hardly different in this respect from René Char's fragment on fire, Celan's text on "for" is in the first place not *poeto*logical but *philo*logical poetry. Celan's poem ascribes to itself, and describes philology as, the movement of the *of*, the *for*, and the *ad*. It is not a transcendental philology, one that would codify the entirety of the movement of language and what it concerns. It does not content itself with the conditions of possibility of a completed linguistic totality but rather pursues the preconditions of philology's working [*Wirken*] and the poem's reality [*Wirklichkeit*]. It works at the seam of the texture out of which a whole could be made, and it works the whole—the work [*das Werk*]—*as* a seam. It does not subject itself to the accepted forms of language but rather intervenes in their inventory by paronomastically altering *Antworten* into *Entworten*, "answering" into an "unwording," and with this alteration it brings to language the *withdrawal* of the word from language rather than a mere variation of the word. It makes it clear that every word is open to other words and all words to none. It does not present itself as the leading and parent science of all possible others but rather as an idiosyncratic praxis that leads, through contravention and deviance, to a zero point of knowledge—the point of origin and the indifference point of reflection—at which every guarantee to protection by conventions is abandoned and the ambition to be ascribed to knowledge, even the knowledge of knowledge, is given up as well. Philology speaks *for* the forms, the transcendentals of violence, language, and image. Speaking in this way *for* them, it does not speak *in* forms or in ways appropriate to forms but rather contradicts and *contraimages* them and deprives them of itself; therefore, it remains the contratranscendental philology, the of-, *for-*, and *ad*transcendental philology that must both work against every philology decreed, and precede every projected one, as transcendental. It is the absolute form, the critical "form" of all forms—their blinding, as Benjamin writes—the form that itself does not preserve any form and that cannot be defined by a higher one. If it can be characterized as a transcendental philology, then only corresponding to the Schelgelian definition of poesy as *progressive*, which is always underway and never reaches the goal of a totality of the conditions of the productions of its acts and rules. Just as violence *unwields* in order to take effect, it does not act, least of all "performatively," but rather *deacts* [*enthandelt*]. Violence never just brings about speech acts, in which conventions of behavior yet again consolidate themselves; rather, it sets in motion the event of an *Ent-sprechung*, an unworking of speech and correspondence that renders all conventions powerless. Violence thus deactivates not only its individual speech acts by placing these acts under the provision of a mere approximation and "treatment" of objects, themes, and histories—an approach that for some time has been called "interpretation" without being called into question—it moreover deactivates the rules of action under which it works, by exposing these rules as historical variables in further alterations, transformations, and thus erasures. Violence *works* by weaving together these forms and their dissolution. Therefore, it is a movement as *trans*formative as it is *ad*formative and *a*formative. As an advocatorial praxis, philology cannot be interested in generalizations without making clear that they speak *for* a hypergeneral, be it even a singular one. Philology must in each case highlight, in the individual phenomena to which it attends, what works *for* a supraindividual—be it even one that balks at generalizations. In each of its gestures, it is a question of "for," understood as an "above and beyond," and in every "for" it is a question of the furthering of philology. Philology is the advocate of infinitization, whether into the most miscroscopic or the macroscopic. *For* everything and for nothing, philology is *more* than everything and nothing. Only philology admits this, but at the same time it grants admission to other possibilities and therein the possibility of not being able to speak for this other with the same "for."

Celan's line about unwording in "for" is not only an answer to Benjamin's reflections on the critique of violence and on the concept of art criticism in German romanticism, and it is also more than just an answer to Dostoevsky's *The Idiot*, the Hassidic stories, and the fragments of Novalis. At the same time it is an answer to every word of his own text and within that word to all of language. It speaks only by placing the already spoken into other relationships, by relinquishing what has been thus transformed to "mere speaking" and simply continuing to speak, and by making space in its "for" for other meanings than those initially intended by Benjamin, Dostoevsky, and Novalis. It speaks for other languages, those of the possible reader, and it speaks by speaking against the violence of—and in—the word, for something other than language. The philology that this reader practices is a philology of anti- and ante-words [*Antworten*] to this other and a philology of unwording [*Entworten*] for the benefit of *other* others. Not by falling mute does the unwording of philology betray language but rather by exposing those features in the structure of language in which, in order to be able to become a language for others and still others, it ceases to be merely *a* language and merely the language of *a* speaker; in those others language itself falls mute, in order to provide access for something other than language and to a language other than this one. One of the most constitutive and deconstitutive features of every responsive, responsible, and—in its emphatic sense—philological language is thereby designated: it speaks for the *epoché* of language, images, and their violence, and it speaks from this *epoché* in order to speak for another and thus in order to be able to speak in the first place. The "for" is this *epoché* of language. It renders it usable for another and only in this way suitable for language. "It unwords in the for"—in a "for" for the benefit of a for that *re*sponds to a language that does not yet exist and perhaps never will. Philology says a word for this "for."

The minimal answer to the question of what a philological question is can therefore only read: *every one*—and above all, the one that pursues the movement of questioning and in it discloses what exceeds every given language. A philological question is everything that speaks for speaking and continuing to speak, that speaks for the languages of others and for something other than languages, and that lets this and itself—ad infinitum—come to language. A philological question is the gate—an opening: the "for"—that lets language pass.

There has not always been such a gate. It can fall shut, it can become obstructed, it can collapse.

One more time: philology sets forth [*setzt . . . fort*]. It sets forth and unfolds what for it is given in insufficient determinacy yet nevertheless as determinable, and it must therefore return again and again to that from which it departs, and at the same time it must return to that from which what for it was pregiven has parted. Philology is, to the extent that it is a setting forth and continuing onward and an unfolding, repetition. But even before it can be the repetition of a given word or work, it must be a repetition of the distance from which it receives this given word and gives it an answer, the distance from which this given word itself became either an answer to a word that preceded it or even an answer to no word. Philology is thus not only the unfolding of a given word in its repetition, nor is it the continuation or even the fulfillment of its promise; philology is in the first place and before all else the repetition of the distance that separates its word from every earlier one, and even this word from its predecessors. As much as it professes a love of language, philology in the first place is the continually repeated experience of the separation from language. Hence the antiphilological affect. It directs itself against the repetition of the pain of not being able to abide by what is already said or what is being said but instead having to return to what is therein inaccessible and threatening for linguistic being [*sprachliches Dasein*]. In *every* word philology must confront the danger that *this* word is not the one and perhaps *no* word is; in every meaning it must confront the threat that it is other than the one meant and *in limine* that it could have no meaning. Hardly a tendency is more widespread in the "historical philological disciplines" than the construction of impenetrable systems of explanation to defend against this threat, systems that are supposed to make superfluous both every loss of speech or intention and every repetition of this loss, which, after all, are constitutive for language. Should philology subject itself to such a system, it will become the armor against the very divisions to which it owes its existence, and it will remain, even under the façade of a stupefying eloquence, the mute secretary of a stammering administrator.

Philology begins by beginning *again*. It takes up the movement of language in the moment in which it releases itself from an earlier language and sets out to become a new one. In the interval between an abandoned and an inconclusive language, between a setting aside and a setting off, it commences this movement: not the movement of a language but rather the movement of a leap of language, and not the movements of two languages but rather the pause in the interval between them. Philology, along with language and its historical time, originates in the hollow between languages. If philology is the repetition of both the step toward a language and the step away from an earlier one, then it is the repetition of that pause of languages and therefore the repetition of that which itself can be neither language nor its object. Philology is the repetition of that which never was. Philology takes up what never was, and it takes with it everything that originates from it and everything that escapes from it—including what bears the appearance of the most solid facticity—into the intermittent movement of its language. Because it is the repetition [*Wiederhohlung*] of the interval of languages, it is both their and its own repeated hollowing out [*Wieder-*

höhlung]. Only thus emptied does philology offer language a "for" for every *pro* and every *contra*, a "for" for the history of what has been and for others that still may be to come. It offers this "nothing" that makes something "usable," about which Benjamin, citing Rosenzweig, speaks in his essay on Kafka.

Accordingly philology "receives" [*empfängt*] not only what for it is pregiven. Since philology, beyond what is given, always also takes up and brings to language what is lacking in all empirical inventories, and since philology can register what is lacking only as other than a factum and can receive what is lacking only as other than a datum, it must, corresponding [*entsprechend*] to the nongivenness of what is lacking, *set loose* [*ent-fangen*] what it receives [*empfangen*]. The logical affect of philology cannot be a vaguely passive sense for what is missing, and it cannot be a sensibility [*Empfindug*] for things recovered [*Aufgefundenens*] or yet to be retrieved [*Wiederzufindendes*]. It must be far more an *Ent-findung*, a *sans-ibility* for that which can neither be found nor founded. This unworking of reception, this *Entfängnis*, is the gesture of philology, just as this "sans-ibility," and not the affected pathos of a "sensibility," is the affect of philology. With it philology *answers* by *unwording*, and in this way even its answers to the concepts that are supposed to say what it does are an unworking of those concepts, starting with that of the answer.

NOTES

PART I: REFERENCES (BY THESIS NUMBER)

[Citations refer to published English translations when available. Translations silently modified throughout. All notes to this section were added by the translator.]

8. Aristotle, *De interpretatione*, 26, in *Complete Works*, ed. Jonathan Barnes (Princeton, N.J.: Princeton University Press, 1984), 1:641–692.

27. Novalis, "Monolog," in *Werke*, 4th ed., ed. Gerhard Schulz (Munich: C. H. Beck, 2001), 426. "Monologue," in *Philosophical Writings*, trans. and ed. Margaret Mahony Stoljar (Albany, N.Y.: SUNY Press, 1997), 83.

30. Nietzsche, "Encyclopädie der Philologie," in *Nietzsche Werke. Kritische Gesamtausgabe*, ed. Giorgio Colli, Mazzino Montinari, et al. (Berlin: de Gruyter, 1967–), pt. 1, vol. 5, p. 193.

41. Alois Riegl, *Late Roman Art Industry*, trans. Rolf Winkes (Rome: Bretschneider, 1985), 229.

42. Ungaretti, "Mattina," in *Vita d'un uomo: tutte le poesie*, ed. Leone Piccioni (Milan: Mondadori, 1969), 65.

50. Friedrich Hölderlin, "In lieblicher Bläue . . ./In lovely blue . . . ," in *Hymns and Fragments*, trans. Richard Sieburth (Princeton, N.J.: Princeton University Press, 1984), 250–251.

52. Paul Celan, "Tübingen, Jänner," in *Die Gedichte: Kommentierte Gesamtausgabe in einem Band*, ed. Barbara Wiedemann (Frankfurt am Main: Suhrkamp, 2005), 133. "Tübingen, January," in *Poems of Paul Celan* (New York: Persea, 1988), 177.

54. Roman Jakobson, "Linguistics and Poetics," in *Language in Literature*, ed. Krystyna Pomorska and Stephen Rudy (Cambridge, Mass.: Harvard University Press, 1987), 69–71.

61. Blaise Pascal, *Pensées*, in *Oeuvres complètes*, ed. Louis Lafuma (Paris: Seuil, 1963), 493–640, frag. 41.

65. Paul Verlaine, "Art poétique," in *Oeuvres poétiques complètes*, ed. Jacques Borel (Paris: Gallimard, 1962), 326–327. Shakespeare, *Hamlet*, 5.2.310.

76. Sigmund Freud, *The Complete Letters of Sigmund Freud to Wilhelm Fliess, 1887–1904*, trans. and ed. Jeffrey Masson (Cambridge, Mass.: Harvard University Press, 1985), 290.

84. Sigmund Freud, *The Complete Letters of Sigmund Freud to Wilhelm Fliess, 1887–1904*, trans. and ed. Jeffrey Masson (Cambridge, Mass.: Harvard University Press, 1985), 287.

92. Wilhelm Waiblinger, "Friedrich Hölderlins Leben, Dichtung, und Wahnsinn," in *Sämtliche Werke: Große Stuttgarter Ausgabe*, by Friedrich Hölderlin, ed. Friedrich Beißer et al. (Stuttgart: Kohlhammer, 1946–1985), vol. 7.3, p. 66.

95. Franz Kafka, "Konvolut 1920," in *Kritische Ausgabe: Nachgelassene Schriften und Fragmente*, ed. Jürgen Born et al. (Frankfurt am Main: Fischer, 1992), 2:354.

This work is reprinted from "95 Theses on Philology" (*PMLA* 125) and appears with permission of the Modern Language Association of America. It was orignally published by Urs Engeler as Roughbooks 008: Werner Hamacher, *95 Thesen zur Philologie* (Frankfurt am Main: Holderbank, 2010).

PART II

Translator's note: This translation has benefited immensely from the close attention of Paul North and Nina Berfelde.

1. [Translator's note: The word *Verändertes* itself is deformed, mispronounced, altered, an *a* substituted for the historically habitual *ä*.]

2. [Translator's note: *Sich selbst vorweg bei sich als bei Anderem.* A modification of the temporal character of Dasein as care from Heidegger's *Being and Time*, "*sich vorweg im schon sein in einer Welt als sein-bei* (*innerweltlichem Seienden*)."]

3. [Translator's note: The reference here and above is to the famous opening lines of Kant's 1784 essay "Answer to the Question: What Is the Enlightenment?" [*Beantwortung der Frage: Was ist Aufklärung?*]

4. Cited according to the *Kritische Friedrich-Schlegel-Ausgabe*, 2:241.

5. Ibid., 16:72 (no. 21).

6. Ibid., 16:68 (no. 80).

7. Ibid., 18:106 (no. 929).

8. Ibid., 18:84 (no. 651).

9. Compare with ibid., 18:81 (no. 624).

10. Ibid. 18:83 (no. 641).

11. Ibid., 18:85 (no. 668).

12. Ibid., 2:168 (no. 22).

13. René Char, *Œuvres completes*, 377.

14. The reference to this can be found in Eric Marty's *René Char*, 174, as well as in Horst Wernicke, "'Die Bibliothek in Flammen': René Chars Dichtung des Aufbruchs," 263ff.) Horst Wernicke was kind enough to tell me that René Char, in a conversation with him, had drawn attention to the connection between the poem title and the codeword of the resistance. Furthermore, he reports that in the resistance museum in Fontaine-de-Vaucluse, which Char helped to build, there is a tattered notebook containing all of the codewords for the battles from then and that even this codeword is printed in it (letter from February 8, 2005).

15. Paul Celan, *Die Gedichte aus dem Nachlass*, 214.

16. Walter Benjamin, *Gesammelte Schriften*, 1:56. See also Walter Benjamin, *Selected Writings*, vol. 4, *1938–1940*, 146. On Celan's reading notes in his edition of Benjamin's artwork criticism study, compare Alexandra Richter, Patrik Alac, and Bertrand Badiou, eds., *Paul Celan—La Bibliothèque philosophique*, 302–303. The reading of "Against a Masterpiece" (*Wider ein Meisterwerk*) from the second volume of Benjamin's *Schriften*, in which the study on the concept of art criticism also is located, is dated August 19, 1968 (ibid., 287). Of the poems that were listed on the same day as "Und wie die Gewalt," it can be shown that they likewise take up motifs from Benjamin's artwork study and from texts of the same volume of the *Schriften*. Accordingly, "Übermeister,/du unterst/nach oben" (Celan, *Die Gedichte aus dem Nachlass*, 215) is a reply to a statement of Schlegel, cited by Benjamin, in which he designates his Athenaeum essay "Über Goethes Meister" as the "Übermeister." This poem too pursues the structure of reflection and the structure of the medium of reflection.

17. Benjamin, *Gesammelte Schriften*, 1:58. See also Benjamin, *Selected Writings*, 4:147.

18. A connection to the following observation by Lichtenberg is thinkable: "If acumen is a magnifying glass, wit is a minifying glass. Do you

believe that discoveries can be made solely with magnifying glasses? I believe that with minifying glasses, or at least with similar instruments in the intellectual world, more discoveries have been made. Through a telescope turned around, the moon looks like Venus, and with the naked eye it looks like Venus through a good one in its correct position. Through an ordinary pair of opera glasses the Pleiades would look like a supernova. The world, which is so beautifully covered with trees and vegetation, contains a higher being than the one that for us appears mouldy. The most beautiful star-filled heaven, seen through a telescope turned around, looks empty." [D 469] (Georg Ch. Lichtenberg, *Schriften und Briefe*, 301.)—My thanks go to Clara Hendriks for the reference to this passage.

19. Celan, *Die Gedichte aus dem Nachlass*, 213: "DU, MICHAELA, [. . .] Du, Aura [. . .] du Wissend-Unwissende,/am Indifferenzpunkt/der Reflexion/[. . .]." To clarify the concepts of "reflection" and "point of indifference," Baraba Wiedemann gives a reference to a textbook of physiology. This note, made in the collected edition of Celan's poems that she has commentated and edited, are not devalued but rather expanded through the connection of these verses to Benjamin.

20. Benjamin, *Gesammelte Schriften*, 1:63. Cf. 1:39.

21. [Translator's note: The German verb *wirken*, cognate with the English "to work," can also mean in German "to weave," as well as "to have effects" or "to take effect." In the following pages, however, *wirken* is worked into the translation primarily in the form of the verb "to work" not only because, as Hamacher explicitly states, it cannot be identified with only having or taking causal "effects" but also because it is important to keep in play the lexical proximity of *wirkt/works*, as "work" thereby becomes a point of indifference, a word of transition between the two languages in which the one receives, unwords, and unworks the other.]

22. Benjamin, *Gesammelte Schriften*, 1:119. See also Walter Benjamin, *Selected Works*, vol. 1, *1913–1926*, ed. Michael Jennings and Marcus Bullock (Cambridge, Mass.: Harvard University Press, 1997), 185.

23. Further remarks on this "mutation" can be found in my essay "Häm—Ein Gedicht Celan mit Motiven Benjamins," in *Jüdisches Denken in einer Welt ohne Gott. Festschrift für Stéphane Mosès*, ed. Mattern, Motzkin, and Sandbank (Berlin: Vorwerk, 2001), 173–197.

24. What is present in these verses as the Christian's kiss on the *seam*

[*Saum*] of the mantle-devotions of the Hassidic rabbi from Martin Buber's "The Legend of the Baal-Shem" may also be reminiscent of the well-known note in which Kafka reflects on what he missed out on [*Versäumten*] and remarks: "I have not been led into life by the—admittedly already slack and falling—hand of Christianity as Kierkegaard was, and have not caught the hem of the Jewish prayer shawl [*Gebetsmantel*], as the Zionists have. I am end or beginning." Franz Kafka, *Nachgelassene Schriften und Fragmente*, 2:98.